super.activ

TENNIS

Anita Ganeri

Illustrated by Karen Donnelly

Consultant: Simon Ickringill, Tennis
Professional at Ilkley Lawn Tennis
and Squash Club, Registered LTA Pro.

Hodder
Children's
Books

a division of Hodder Headline

To Clare AG

Text copyright 2000 © Anita Ganeri
Illustrations copyright 2000 © Karen Donnelly
Published by Hodder Children's Books 2000

Designed by Fiona Webb
Series designed by Fiona Webb

10 9 8 7 6 5 4 3 2 1

A catalogue record for this book is available from the British Library.

ISBN: 0340 76446 5

Printed by Clays Ltd, St Ives plc

Hodder Children's Books
a division of Hodder Headline
338 Euston Road
London NW1 3BH

J114,727
£3.99

Meet the author

Anita Ganeri has won Wimbledon twice... in her dreams! The closest she's really ever got to lifting a cup on Centre Court is having a mug of tea and a sandwich when rain stopped play. Instead, she has to content herself with playing twice a week for her local club where her enthusiastic (though not always accurate) groundstrokes have her opponents running for cover. She also watches as much tennis as possible on TV and whenever time allows, likes to travel to tennis tournaments to stock up on souvenirs. Her collection of wristbands is second to none.

Apart from her efforts to play, in addition to writing this book, Anita is the author of another book on tennis skills which she wrote with the help of David Lloyd. Happily, he has now recovered from the experience and has gone on to bigger and better things as captain of Britain's Davis Cup team. So Anita knows what she *should* be doing, if only the net didn't always seem to get in the way...

Introduction

You may not have a serve like Greg Rusedski or a forehand to match Pete Sampras but if you know one end of a tennis racket from the other, there's hope for you yet. With a few basic pointers and plenty of practice, anyone can take part in the most exciting, rewarding – and frustrating game in the world. Whether you want to play a friendly knock-around, or have dreams of reaching a Grand Slam final, this is the book for you. See how to set a match sizzling with your topspin forehand, dazzle your friends with your delicate dropshots and tantalise your opponents with your razor-sharp grasp of tactics. Inside are tonnes of coaching tips to help you play like a pro.

And remember, tennis needn't cost you (or your parents) a fortune. All you need to start with is a borrowed racket and a ball. Then get yourself down to your local park and start grooving your groundstrokes. But be warned! Once you start playing tennis, you'll be hooked!

Anita

Contents

Anyone for tennis?

If you've been watching tennis on TV, you might think that tennis today is all about whacking the ball as hard as you can, using the latest in racket technology, and grunting loudly. But it wasn't always like this. In fact, tennis had much more regal beginnings.

Real tennis

A game like tennis was first played in France in the 13th century by some sport-loving monks. It was played over a net on a court like a squash court, based on the shape of the monastery cloisters. The aim of the game was to hit the ball over the net and to make it rebound off the walls. The game later became popular with the royal family, and came to be known as 'real' or 'royal' tennis. It's still sometimes played today.

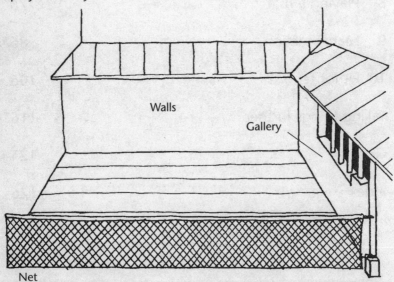

Walls

Gallery

Net

A sticky start?

In the 19th century, people tried to invent a version of real tennis which could be played outside on a lawn. In 1874, Major Walter Clopton Wingfield introduced a very popular type of tennis called sphairistike, or 'sticky' for short. Played on a court shaped like an hourglass with the net stretched across the narrow bit in the middle, the game was soon re-named 'lawn tennis'.

Pro tennis

The first tennis championships were held at the All England Croquet and Lawn Tennis Club at Wimbledon, London, in 1877, on a new rectangular court. Just 200 spectators watched the men's final (women didn't play until 1884), a far cry from the 15,000 that pack Centre Court today. From then on, there was no stopping tennis and it was soon being played all over the world.

For today's top players, tennis is a full-time job, earning them fortunes in prize money and sponsorship. But even Pete Sampras and Martina Hingis had to start somewhere...

Tennis kit

All you need to start playing tennis is a racket, a ball and a friend to hit with. At this stage, you can wear your ordinary school games kit, but if you want to go further and join a club, you'll need to splash out on some proper tennis gear. It doesn't need to be expensive, but it must be comfortable and allow you to move easily about the court.

Choosing shoes

Running, changing direction and braking on court all put great strain on your feet, so a good pair of tennis shoes is essential – ask any player who's suffered from blisters! Buy shoes that are specially designed for tennis (squash or running shoes will not do), and always replace them when they wear out. Look for the following features when choosing your shoes:

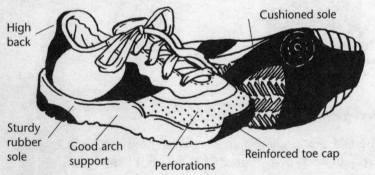

High back

Cushioned sole

Sturdy rubber sole

Good arch support

Perforations

Reinforced toe cap

Clothes

The traditional colour for tennis is white and as some clubs still won't let you wear coloured clothing, make sure you check out the rules. Choose clothes made from light, natural materials such as cotton which is good at absorbing sweat. Most girls wear tennis dresses, or skirts and shirts. Most boys wear shorts and shirts. The next page lists some other things you will need.

• Socks
Choose thick, towelling socks to cushion your feet and soak up sweat. Some players wear two pairs for extra padding.

• Wristbands
Wear towelling wristbands to soak up sweat and stop it trickling down your racket arm on to your hand.

• Tracksuit
Make sure you wear a tracksuit while you're warming up or waiting for your game to begin. You should be able to slip the tracksuit bottoms easily over your shoes. Always put the tracksuit on again after playing to avoid pulling a muscle by cooling down too quickly.

• Headband
A headband is useful for keeping your hair off your face and for stopping sweat running into your eyes.

• Tennis bag
A strong, lightweight bag is needed for carrying your kit. You can buy sports bags large enough to fit a racket inside.

What a racket

Remember the tennis-mad monks? They called their game 'jeu de paume' ('game of the palm') because they hit the ball with the palms of their hands. Ouch! To save their skin, players later wore leather and string mittens, then wooden paddles instead. It wasn't long before the paddles turned into rackets. Until about 30 years ago, everyone played with a wooden racket. Today new materials such as titanium have left wood way behind, meaning that players can now hit the ball harder than ever. But before you find out which racket is right for you, it's a good idea to get to know rackets better.

Parts of a racket

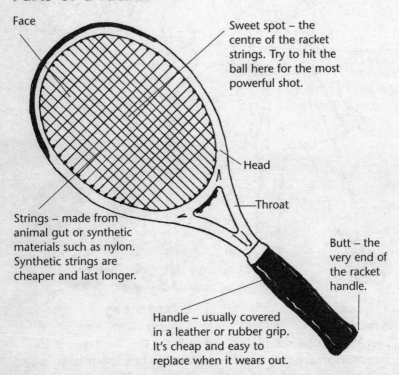

Face

Sweet spot – the centre of the racket strings. Try to hit the ball here for the most powerful shot.

Head

Throat

Strings – made from animal gut or synthetic materials such as nylon. Synthetic strings are cheaper and last longer.

Butt – the very end of the racket handle.

Handle – usually covered in a leather or rubber grip. It's cheap and easy to replace when it wears out.

Choosing the right racket

Go into a good sports shop and you'll be dazzled by the range of rackets on display. So which do you choose? Don't be put off by the jargon or swayed by the adverts which promise to have you playing like the next Tim Henman or Patrick Rafter. First find out if you enjoy playing tennis and what sort of player you are. Then ask your coach or sports shop to suggest a good racket that doesn't cost a fortune.

Coach tips

- It's important to choose the right racket for you. When you play, your racket should feel like a natural extension of your arm.
- Forget titanium to start with. A graphite mix is probably best.
- Rackets come in different weights – a light or medium-light racket is probably best. Try a few practice shots to check that the racket doesn't feel too heavy.
- The bigger the racket head, the bigger the sweet spot, but an oversized head can be hard to control. Try a mid-size for starters.
- The size of the racket handle is called the grip, and it's vital to get the size of the 'grip' right to prevent tennis elbow. When you hold the racket in your hand, your thumb and middle finger should overlap slightly. If in doubt, buy a smaller size rather than a bigger. You can always build it up with tape.

Warming up

Now it's time to get down to some serious work. But before you're let loose on the tennis court, you need to warm up. This means some gentle exercises to get your muscles loose and ready for action – otherwise you risk getting injured.

There are many different warm-up exercises and here are a few for starters. You can do these before a practice or coaching session, but you should add more stretching exercises if you're warming up before a match.

Jogging – jog gently around the court five times, swinging your arms as you go.

Shoulder stretch – bend one arm behind your head. Gently pull back your elbow with your other hand, hold for 20 seconds and swap arms. Do three times on each side.

Leg stretch – sit on the ground with your legs stretched out, feet together and knees flat to the floor. Reach down your legs, as far as you can, with your hands. Hold for 20 seconds, then relax. Do this two more times.

Eating and drinking

It's crucial to keep your energy and fluid levels up before and during a match. Leave at least an hour between eating and playing. Then if you're hungry on court, munch on a banana – they're nutritious and easy to digest. Drink plenty of water or squash.

New balls?

Tennis balls are made from rubber covered in wool or synthetic fabric. The best balls are pressurized (they have air sealed inside), but you'll need to keep replacing them once they lose their bounce. In tournaments, new balls are used every 7, 9 or 11 games.

Practice, practice, practice

You know the old saying "Practice makes perfect"? Well, it's true! By practising hard and often, your game will soon improve. Your shots will start to come automatically so that you don't have to stop and think what to do. With practice you'll be able to spot mistakes and eliminate them from your game. Practice will also make you more consistent which in turn will make you more confident.

Another great way to learn is to watch professionals in action. But don't forget the hours and hours of practice that have gone into making it look so easy!

ACE PRACTICE

Throughout this book, you'll see boxes like this one giving you ideas and tips for practice. Here are a few to start with:

- Practice as you mean to play, giving 100% effort and concentration. You will then carry this over into matches.
- Plan your practice sessions and give each one a purpose, such as concentrating on getting your backhand back deep, or on your return of serve.
- Practice on your own or with a friend. And whatever you do, have fun!

The aim of the game

The aim of tennis is to win points by hitting the ball over the net out of your opponent's reach for an outright winner, or forcing your opponent into making a weak reply or error. Oh, and you must keep the ball in court. Simple!

Left or right-handed?

The instructions in this book are for right-handed players. To suit left-handers, they should be reversed.

2 Ready to play

The court

The days of Major Wingfield's hourglass court are long gone. Today all tennis courts are the same rectangular shape and size, with identical markings which show the limits for your serves, drives and volleys. The lines should be between 2.5–5 cm thick, apart from the baseline which can be up to 10 cm thick.

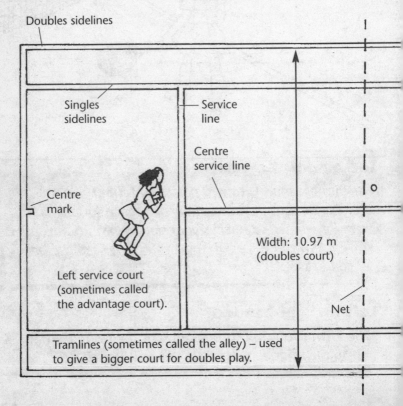

Doubles sidelines

Singles sidelines

Service line

Centre service line

Centre mark

Width: 10.97 m (doubles court)

Left service court (sometimes called the advantage court).

Net

Tramlines (sometimes called the alley) – used to give a bigger court for doubles play.

In the zone

The court is divided into three 'zones' – the backcourt (baseline); the forecourt (between the service line and net) and no-man's land (between the backcourt and the forecourt). Try not to get caught in no-man's land.

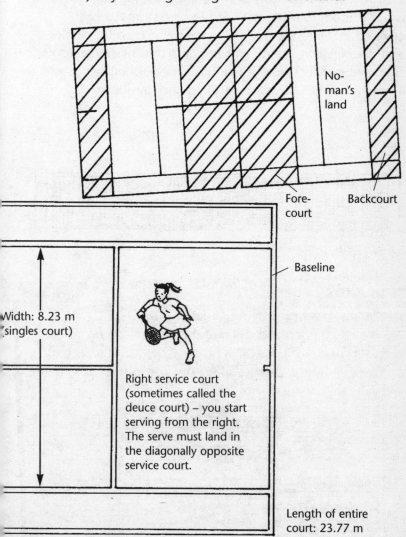

No-man's land

Fore-court

Backcourt

Baseline

Width: 8.23 m (singles court)

Right service court (sometimes called the deuce court) – you start serving from the right. The serve must land in the diagonally opposite service court.

Length of entire court: 23.77 m

The net

The net is stretched across the centre of the court. It's higher at the ends (1.07 m) than in the middle (0.91 m) and is supported at each end by net posts which stand 0.91 m outside the singles or doubles sidelines. The net is suspended from the net cord (a cord or metal cable covered in white tape). If the same net is used for singles and doubles play, 'singles sticks' are put in place for singles. Get used to checking the height of the net before you play – most clubs will have a measuring stick available.

Net post   Net   Net cord   Singles stick

In or out?

The ball is in if any part of it touches the line. It's out if the whole ball bounces outside the line. It can be difficult to call in or out if the ball is hit very hard and fast. If in doubt, play the point again. It will save a lot of needless arguments!

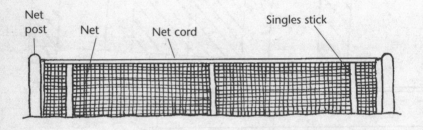

In

Only this ball is out

Out

The umpire

If you're playing with friends, call your own lines. It's up to you to be honest! You'll also have to keep score. In tournament play, the umpire keeps and calls out the score and makes sure that you stick to the rules. Umpires get blamed for everything from ball calls to bad weather, but you should never ever argue with the umpire.

LINE JUDGES

The umpire is helped by line judges who call the ball in or out. Another of their jobs is watching for foot faults.

NET JUDGE

Keeps his or her finger on the net cord to feel if the serve hits the net. If it does and lands in, a 'let' is called.

BALL GIRLS AND BOYS

Collect up balls and supply balls for players to serve with. A great way to watch the action!

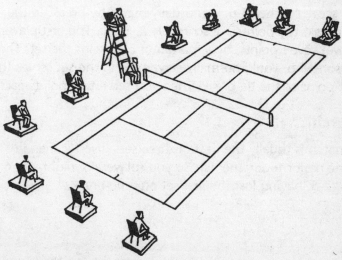

To serve or not to serve?

Before you start knocking up before a match, toss a coin or spin your racket. The player who wins the toss can choose to serve first, receive first or choose which end to play from.

Keeping score

Game...

Tennis scoring may seem strange at first but you'll soon get the hang of it, honestly! A game starts at 0, or 'love'. To win a game, a player must win the next four points, called 15, 30, 40 and game. If the score is 40-40, or deuce, the player must win the next two points, which are called advantage and game.

Set...

The first player to win six games, by a margin of at least two, wins the set. If the score is 5-5, play seven games. If the score reaches 6-6, you usually play a tie-break. In the tie-break, the points are scored 1, 2, 3 etc. The first player to win seven points, by a margin of two, wins the set. The person who would normally serve next in the set serves the first point of the tie-break. Then you serve two points each.

Match...

A match is usually the best of three sets (five for men in some major tournaments). So you (player A) might win 6-7, 6-4, 7-5, having lost the first set on a tie-break.

Ready to play

The server's score
is called out first

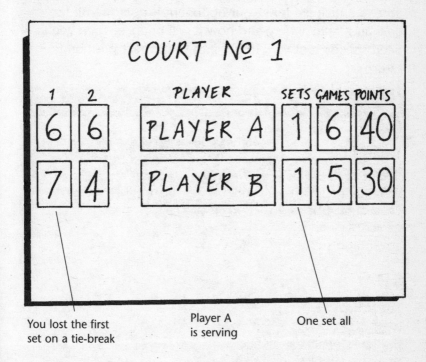

You lost the first
set on a tie-break

Player A
is serving

One set all

*This scoreboard shows you at match point. If you win the next point,
you win the match. Can you handle the pressure?*

Longest match

*Did you know that tie-breaks were brought in to stop
sets becoming too long. This means that you'll never
see another scoreline like 22-24, 1-6, 16-14, 6-3, 11-9.
This was the 1969 Wimbledon men's singles final
when Pancho Gonzales beat Charlie Pasarell.*

Basic skills

Ball sense, balance, coordination and footwork are just as important as good stroke play. With practice, you should be able to anticipate how your opponent is going to hit the ball, and 'read' where and how it will bounce. Then you'll need speedy footwork to get into the correct position to return it.

ACE PRACTICE

To practise hand-eye coordination, stand with a partner about 2 m apart. Then each throw (underarm) a ball to the other at the same time. Watch the ball closely through the air. Try clapping your hands behind your back before you catch the ball, to make it more difficult.

Fancy footwork

Footwork means lining your feet up in the correct position to hit the ball. In a fast-moving match, it's essential for getting into position quickly and keeping your balance as you hit your shots. Watch professional tennis players – they are never still, but are constantly bouncing about on court, ready to move off to the ball.

Are you ready?

Tennis is a fast-moving game so you'll need to be quick off the mark. Be ready to move into position as soon as your opponent hits the ball. To move off quickly in any direction, return to the ready position after each shot you play and for receiving serves.

For the ready position, stand with your feet shoulder-width apart, and your knees slightly bent. Your weight should be forward on the balls of your feet, so you're ready to push off. Hold your racket loosely in a forehand grip, supporting it with your other hand. This makes it easier to change grip if you need to hit a backhand or volley (see page 26 for more about grips).

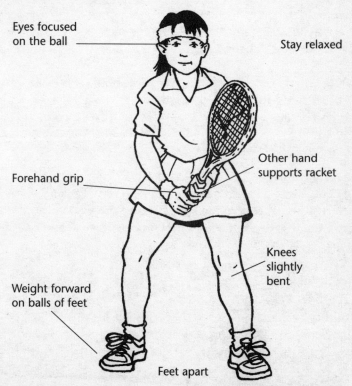

Eyes focused on the ball

Stay relaxed

Forehand grip

Other hand supports racket

Knees slightly bent

Weight forward on balls of feet

Feet apart

The Grand Slam

The four most prestigious tennis tournaments around are the four Grand Slams – the Australian Open, the US Open, the French Open and Wimbledon. To win the Grand Slam of Grand Slams, you must win all four in the same calendar year. Very few players ever achieve this. The last Grand Slam winner was Steffi Graf of Germany in 1988.

The Australian Open

When held: January
Where held: Melbourne Park, Melbourne, Australia
Playing surface: Rebound Ace

Soaring temperatures make the two weeks of the Australian Open a real test for players' strength and stamina. In fact, after his first title in 1991, Germany's Boris Becker threw himself into the river to cool off! It's hot, laid back and it kicks off the tennis year.

The first Australian Open was held in 1905. Since then, it's been held in six different venues, including New Zealand. Its current home, Melbourne Park, has four show courts and a Centre Court with a retractable roof (in case it rains) and seating for 15,000.

Championship points

- *The youngest men's singles champion was Australia's Ken Rosewall. He won the title in 1953, aged 18 years and 2 months. He was also the oldest champion, winning in 1972 at the age of 37 years and 2 months.*

- *The youngest winner of the Australian Open's women's singles was Martina Hingis of Switzerland. She was just 16 years and 3 months old when she won the title in 1997.*

The US Open

When held: August/September
Where held: Flushing Meadow, New York, USA
Playing surface: Hard courts

The heat of New York, the noisy crowds and the endless procession of aeroplanes flying overhead, make the US Open possibly the hardest Grand Slam to win. It's tough out there and a big test of players' concentration. When it first started, the US Open was played on grass.

3 Going for your shots

To play tennis well, you must master the basic strokes, playing and practising them until you can hit them in your sleep. Solid forehands, backhands, serves and volleys are a tennis player's bread-and-butter, so they must be shots you can really rely on. Once you've got the basics right, you can progress to half-volleys and topspin lobs.

The three main types of shot are groundstrokes, overheads (serves and smashes) and volleys. Shots played to your right are forehands. Shots played to your left are backhands. (Reverse this for left-handers.)

GETTING TO GRIPS

The way you hold your racket is called your grip.
You need to learn the correct grip for each shot and
remember to change your grip between shots. In this book,
each grip is explained with the relevant shot. Grip the
racket near the end of the handle, firmly but not too tightly.

The five basic skills

Here are the five basic skills you'll need to develop a match-winning technique:

1 Watch the ball – from the minute it leaves your opponent's racket until you hit it.
2 Good footwork – to reach and hit the ball, and for quick recovery in readiness for the next shot.
3 Good balance – especially as you hit the ball, to ensure that your shot is controlled.
4 Good racket control – swing the racket at the ball for groundstrokes, a throw for overheads and a punch for volleys.
5 Good racket face control – the angle at which the racket face hits the ball determines where the ball will bounce.

Three steps to good strokes

A stroke is the action of hitting the ball with your racket. There are three main stages to hitting a good stroke – concentrate on each stage as you play a shot.

2 Hit

1 Preparation or take-back

3 Follow-through

ACE PRACTICE

The follow-through helps guide the ball to its target. If you don't follow through properly, you may lose control of the shot. To practise, imagine that you are hitting four balls in a row. Swing your racket through, starting low and ending high. (You need to shorten your follow-through for volleys – see pages 49 and 50.)

Groundstrokes

Groundstrokes are long strokes played after the ball has
bounced. The two main groundstrokes are the forehand
and backhand drives.

The forehand drive

1 From the ready position,
   take your racket back,
   turning sideways on
   your right foot. At the
   same time, turn your
   shoulders round in line
   with the ball.

2 Start to swing your
   racket forwards, stepping
   in with your left foot to
   transfer your weight
   forwards.

3 Hit through the ball at
   about waist height, a
   comfortable distance in
   front of your body.
   Keep your wrist firm
   and swing your hitting
   shoulder in the direction
   of the target.

4 Follow through so that
   your racket finishes up
   by your left shoulder
   and your right elbow is
   pointing at the target.
   Then return to the
   ready position.

GETTING TO GRIPS

Use the eastern forehand or 'shake hands' grip. You need to line up the 'V' between your fingers and thumb with the right-hand ridge on your racket handle.

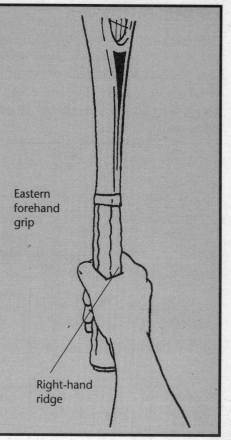

Eastern forehand grip

Right-hand ridge

HOT SHOTS

Pete Sampras (USA) has one of the most feared forehands in men's tennis. Combined with strength, athleticism and a superb all-court game, it has helped him to become one of the greatest tennis players of all time. With a total of 12 Grand Slam titles to his name, including six Wimbledons in seven years, Sampras is the only player to have been world number one for six years in a row.

Forehand tactics

The forehand is useful for returning serves and for playing rallies from the baseline. Aim some shots deep down the line to the back of the court to push your opponent back to the baseline and to give them less time to play a strong reply. Play others 'cross court' at an angle to pull your opponent out wide.

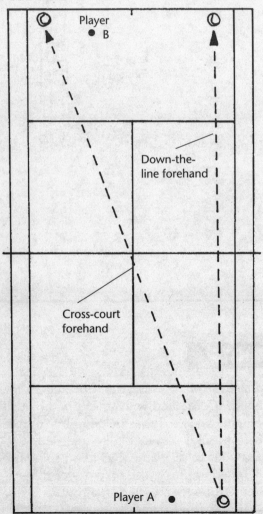

Player B

Down-the-line forehand

Cross-court forehand

Player A

Coach tips

- Try to hit the ball a comfortable
distance from your body so that you're
not hunched up or overstretched.
Hit the ball just in front of your body,
between knee and waist height.
This will give you room to play.
- Stretch out your free hand for balance as you hit.
- Swing your racket through the ball from low to high,
accelerating the racket head as you hit.
- To avoid hitting the ball into the net, aim the ball at least
two nets high whilst you are still learning, to lift it over
the net. If you can, extend a rope or string about a metre
above the net and aim to hit over it. You can take more
risks as you improve.

Groundstrokes are the most commonly played shots, so
you need to be able to rely on them. The only way to learn
to play groundstrokes with confidence, consistency and
accuracy, is to practise.

ACE PRACTICE

To practise groundstrokes on
your own, chalk a line on a wall
at net height. Then chalk some
circles above it at different
heights. Aim for these circles,
first with your forehand, then
backhand, to improve your aim
and accuracy.

The backhand drive

Many players find forehands easier to play than backhands as the forehand somehow seems an easier, more natural stroke. But keep practising! If your opponent sees that you've got a weak backhand, he or she will pile the pressure on by constantly hitting balls to your backhand side. Don't be tempted to run around your backhand and try to hit a forehand – your opponent will exploit this weakness too.

Playing a backhand

1 From the ready position, turn sideways on your left foot. Take your racket back, using your left hand to support it. Change grip as you turn.

2 With your back almost facing the net, start to bring your racket for-wards. At the same time, step in with your right foot to transfer your weight forwards.

3 Swing your racket head at the ball in a long, flowing movement, from low to high.

4 Follow through high towards your target so that your racket finishes high to your right. Then return to the ready position.

GETTING TO GRIPS

Use the eastern
backhand grip.
You can find this by
lining up the 'V' between
your fingers and thumb
with the left-hand plane
on your racket handle.
Don't forget to change
grips between forehands
and backhands.

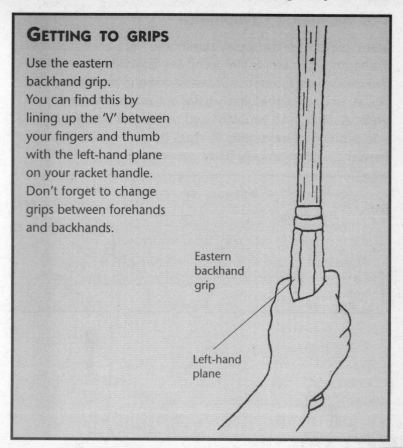

Eastern
backhand
grip

Left-hand
plane

HOT SHOTS

Try modelling your backhand on Tim Henman's. Watch
how he pulls his shoulders round, ready to swing through
the ball. Solid groundstrokes have helped make Henman
Britain's top player, along with Greg Rusedski. Henman's
dream is to win Wimbledon, a venue he first visited as a
five year old! Wimbledon certainly runs in the family –
his grandfather, grandmother and great grandmother
all played at the Championships.

Double-handed backhand

Some players prefer to play backhands with both hands on the racket. This allows you to hit the ball with more power and control as you put your whole weight behind the shot. The down side is that you'll have less reach than with a single-hander. And you will need to recover and get back into position more quickly to react to the next ball. The answer is – learn to play both!

GETTING TO GRIPS

To find the grip for a double-handed backhand, first hold the racket in your right hand as you would for a single-handed backhand. Then place your left hand above it in a left-handed forehand grip. It should be touching your right hand.

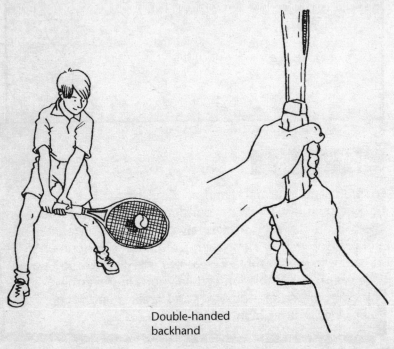

Double-handed
backhand

A firm wrist

It is important to work on your overall fitness for all aspects of tennis, but it is particularly vital that you have strong wrists, especially for backhands. Unless you keep your wrist firm as you hit your backhand, the ball will end up going out or into the net. To strengthen your wrist, squeeze an old tennis ball in your hand. Do this 30 times a day and you'll soon notice a difference!

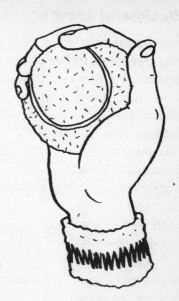

Coach tips

- Use your free hand to help pull your shoulders right round to play a backhand. You should hit the ball with your back almost facing the net.
- Try not to rush your shot or swipe wildly at the ball. Play with intention and control. If you find that you're rushing, slow your swing down and use good footwork to reach the ball.
- Stepping into the ball with your front foot and transferring your weight forwards, adds power to your shots.
- Hitting the ball sideways on adds greater weight and power to your shots. But it isn't always possible. Sometimes you may need to hit with an 'open' stance, with your weight on your back foot.

Backhand tactics

Use backhands like forehands for returning serves and building up rallies. Add topspin to play 'passing shots' which speed past opponents as they come to the net. Add slice to turn them into approach shots. These will allow you to come to the net to play an attacking volley. See chapter 7 for more about topspin and slice.

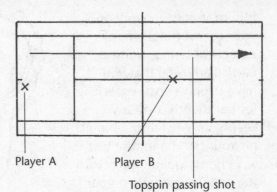

Player A   Player B

Topspin passing shot

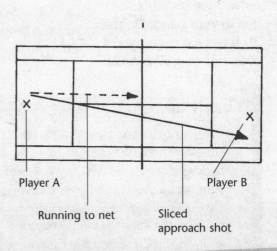

Player A   Player B

Running to net   Sliced
                        approach shot

HOT SHOTS

Monica Seles (USA) uses two hands to play both forehands and backhands. This allows her to play with great power and aggression from the back of the court, as she 'nails' the lines with pinpoint accuracy. Seles is naturally left-handed but the way she plays makes reading her shots doubly difficult for opponents.

Practising groundstrokes

Practising your groundstrokes with a friend will help you
learn to react quickly when the ball is coming towards you.

ACE PRACTICE

With a friend, practise changing the direction of your shots as
you would in a rally. Hit four shots cross court, then your fifth
shot down the line. One of you should hit forehands and the
other backhands. Then change over. Start with 10 shots each,
then build up to 20 shots. See how long you can keep a rally
going for.

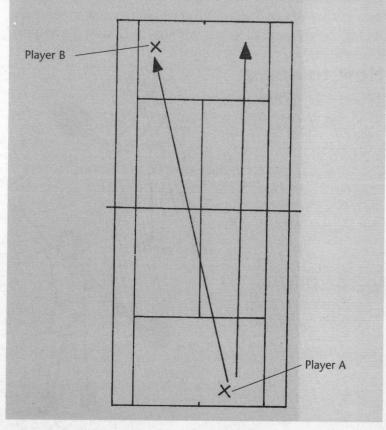

Player B

Player A

Sensational serving

The serve, or service, is the most important shot in tennis. It's the only time when you're in complete control – so you need to make the most of it. You need serves that are fast, accurate and hopefully, unreturnable to put your opponent under pressure and give you a head start.

A good serve is a great weapon to have. Ignore those who say men's tennis is boring because of all those big, booming serves. They're just jealous! Who wouldn't want to serve like Philippousis, Rusedski, Venus Williams or Lindsay Davenport?

How to serve

1 Stand sideways to the net, feet slightly apart. Hold the ball in your left hand.

2 Lower the racket and ball together, keeping your eyes focused on your target.

3 Toss the ball up with your left
   hand. At the same time, take
   your racket round and behind
   your back, as though you are
   scratching your back with
   your racket. Bend your knees.

4 Bring your racket up, behind
   your head, and throw it
   forward to hit the ball.
   Make sure you straighten
   your knees so that you hit
   the ball at full stretch.

5 Follow through in the
   direction of the ball,
   transferring your weight
   into the direction of the shot.
   Finish with your racket down
   by your left side and get
   ready to play the next shot.

GETTING TO GRIPS

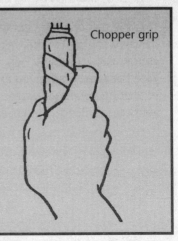

Chopper grip

Use the 'chopper' grip for serving. Hold your racket as if you were holding an axe. If you find this difficult, start off serving with the eastern forehand grip until you feel more confident. Do not grip the racket too tightly.

Where to stand

To serve in singles, stand just behind the baseline, slightly to one side of the centre mark. (In doubles, stand midway between the centre mark and the doubles sidelines. See page 88 for more information on this.) Serve into the diagonally-opposite service box, starting from the right. Aim your serve straight down the centre service line, or diagonally and deep into the corners.

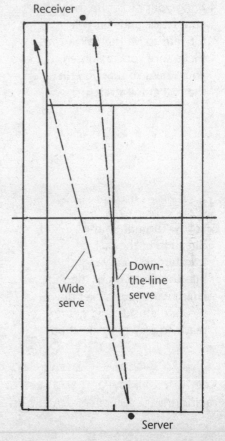

Receiver

Wide serve

Down-the-line serve

Server

HOT SHOTS

Britain's Greg Rusedski has the fastest serve in men's
tennis, regularly blasting down aces at over 200 km/h.
It's a weapon that wins Rusedski plenty of points and can
help him beat anyone in the world. Being left-handed is
a huge advantage – it allows Rusedski to serve into the
body of his opponents, giving them no time to play.

Serve words

- Ace – a winning serve hit so fast and accurately that your
  opponent cannot return it.
- Let – when a point is replayed. If a serve lands in but
  clips the net cord, you play a let.
- Fault – if a serve lands out or in the net.
- Double fault – when both your first and second serves
  fail to go in and your opponent wins the point.
- Foot fault – if your foot touches the baseline or court
  area before you hit the ball (see below).

Underarm serve

Until 1878, everyone served underarm. It's still legal to do
so (*and* you don't have to warn your opponent that you're
about to switch). Only serve underarm in an emergency.
Keep the ball low and add slice to bring your opponent
racing in. (See chapter 7 for more about slice.)

The throw

Getting the ball toss right is crucial to how you serve. Throw the ball up in front of your body, slightly over to your racket side. To make this easier, imagine you are facing a giant clock face. Throw the ball up at 1 o'clock (for right-handers) and 11 o'clock (for left-handers). Aim to hit the ball at full stretch.

If your throw-up goes wrong, you can start again as long as your racket hasn't touched the ball. Don't worry if this happens – even the professionals sometimes have problems. You often hear Australia's Pat Rafter apologising as he gets his ball toss wrong.

ACE PRACTICE

Aim to throw the ball up straight, as if you're throwing it up through a drainpipe. Practise against a corner of your house, or anything with a straight line to guide you.

Second serve

Unlike any other shot in tennis, you get two chances to win a point on your serve. Try to hit a powerful first serve, even though you might put it long or in the net. But don't take risks on your second serve. This doesn't necessarily mean hitting a weak serve, but it must be reliable. Hitting the ball with topspin will give extra control.

Service tactics

Use your serve to put your opponent under pressure right from the start of the game or point. You can't serve aces all the time, but make your serve as tough as possible to return. Keep it deep to force a weak return which can easily be put away for a winner. A strong serve will also make your opponent lose confidence and they will start making mistakes.

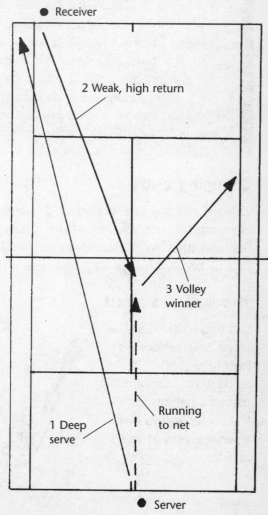

● Receiver

2 Weak, high return

3 Volley winner

Running to net

1 Deep serve

● Server

Coach tips

- Your throw-up and serve should be one long, smooth, continuous action.
- The serve is a throwing action. Accelerate your racket head as you throw it up to the ball.
- Placement is as important as power. Decide where you are going to serve before you throw the ball up.
- Take your time before you serve. Some players bounce the ball a couple of times to help their concentration.
- Keep your head up as you hit the ball. If you drop your head too soon, your shoulders and arm will drop, too, and you'll hit the ball into the net.

Changing ends

To even out any advantages or disadvantages, you alternate the end you serve from. Change ends after the first and then every second game (that is, on odd games). In a tie-break, change ends after every six points.

The ball is served

Did you know that the word 'service' comes from real tennis? In its heyday, a servant tossed a ball up for the server, doing him a service. Now, there's an idea...

Service practice

We've all been there. You're playing a match, and everything's fine, then suddenly your serve goes horribly wrong. Before you know it, your concentration's gone and the rest of your game has fallen apart. Your serve is so crucially important that you can't practise it enough.

ACE PRACTICE 1

'Ghosting' is a good way to practise your serve and check your technique without hitting a ball. Try ghosting your serve in front of a mirror. Can you spot any mistakes? On court, try ghosting a serve, then hitting a serve. Repeat this five times to each service court. Can you feel an improvement?

ACE PRACTICE 2

To improve the accuracy of your serve, line up some targets in the corners of the service boxes. Ball tins are good because they make loads of noise! Aim ten serves at each target. How many times do you manage to hit the tins?

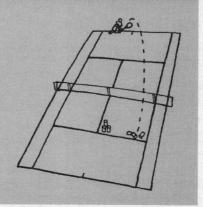

Grand Slam

The French Open'

When held: May/June
Where held: Stade Roland Garros, Paris, France
Playing surface: Red clay

If it's May, it's Paris for the professional tennis tours. And what could be better than playing in a beautiful city on a balmy spring afternoon?

The slow red clay of Paris makes for fascinating duels between the world's best baseliners with their heavy topspin shots. Playing on clay is a speciality, and the tournament often throws up surprise winners. It's a tough place to be an umpire, though. Clay is the only surface where you can see the mark left by the ball and players can ask umpires to get down from their chairs to check if the ball's in or out.

The stadium itself was built in 1928 and is named after World War I French flying ace, Roland Garros. Originally, it had five courts, whereas today it boasts 23 courts, including Centre Court and Court Suzanne Lenglen, named after the legendary French player of the 1920s.

Long rallies mean lots of hanging around for the players, but there are plenty of ways to pass the time. They can play arcade games in the players' restaurant, they can surf the net or chill out and watch their competitors' progress on the banks of television screens. They even have their own hairdresser so that they can look their best for going out on court!

Championship points

- *The first French championships were held in 1891. The women's competition began in 1897.*

- *Suzanne Lenglen was nicknamed 'La Divine' because of her dazzling play. She won the French Open six out of seven times between 1920-1926. The last French player to win the title was Yannick Noah in 1983.*

- *In recent times, the records belong to Bjorn Borg of Sweden, with six singles titles, and Chris Evert of the USA with seven.*

Vicious volleys

A volley is a short, sharp shot played before the ball bounces by punching your racket at the ball. Volleys are attacking shots, played at the net and they give you a great chance of putting the ball away for a clean winner. They're also useful for pushing your opponent back on the defensive.

Even if you prefer to play mostly from the baseline, you should still be able to come to the net and hit a good, solid volley if you need to.

GETTING TO GRIPS

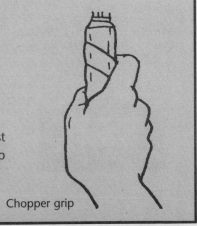

Use the 'chopper' or service grip to play both forehand and backhand volleys. This will save you having to change grips between shots. Squeeze the racket handle just before you hit the ball to keep your wrist firm and to give you greater control.

Chopper grip

The forehand volley

1 Start in the ready position, ready to move off quickly to either side.

2 Turn on your right foot so that you're standing sideways with your left shoulder pointing towards the net. Take your racket back, making sure that you keep your eyes on the ball.

3 Bend your knees and step in with your left foot. Use your left arm to line up the racket head just above the on-coming ball. Punch your racket out in front of you at the ball.

4 Keep the follow-through short and get back into position quickly for the next shot.

Where to stand

For volleys, stand about 2 m from the net. If you stand too far away, you risk hitting the ball into the net. If you are too close to the net, you will not have enough time to react to the on-coming ball and not enough room to get into position. You also risk hitting the net with your racket which will lose you the point.

The backhand volley

1 Start in the ready position, ready to move off quickly to either side.

2 Turn on your left foot so that you're standing sideways with your right shoulder pointing towards the net. Take your racket back, making sure that you keep your eyes on the ball.

3 Bend your knees and step in with your right foot. Use your right arm to line up the racket head just above the on-coming ball. Punch your racket out in front of you at the ball.

4 Keep the follow-through short and get back into position quickly for the next shot.

Double-hander

If you find that your backhand volley is weaker than your forehand, try using two hands on the racket as you would for a double-handed backhand drive.

Highs and lows

Ideally, you should be able to go out and hit perfect volleys time after time, with the ball always reaching you between shoulder and hip height. But tennis isn't always that simple. Get ready to adapt your basic volley for high, low and awkward balls.

High volleys

For high volleys, take your racket back high and punch the ball downwards. Keep your racket head up to avoid hitting the ball into the net.

Low volleys

Bend your knees and keep your body low to get right under the ball. Angle the racket face upwards to lift the ball up and over the net.

Advanced volleys

• DRIVE VOLLEY

A cross between a groundstroke and a volley, useful for attacking short, shoulder-high balls and disrupting your opponent's rhythm. Use your usual groundstroke grips.

• STOP VOLLEY

A stop volley takes the pace (speed) off the ball and makes it drop into your opponent's court where it stops short. Useful if your opponent is stuck behind the baseline.

Half volley

A half-volley is a shot played just after the ball has bounced. It's a tricky shot to pull off but useful if you're caught mid-court with the ball at your feet. Bend your knees and get down low to play the ball. Keep your back straight and your wrist firm. Your grip should be firm but relaxed for better 'feel'.

HOT SHOTS

Pat Rafter (Australia) is famous for his spectacular serve-and-volley game. Rated as one of the best volleyers in the men's game, his strength and athleticism allow him to cover the net so brilliantly that it's tough for opponents to squeeze passing shots by him.

Volley tactics

Getting to the net is a clever tactic. It puts your opponent under pressure to play a passing shot (which may easily go out) or a lob (which you may be able to smash). Come into the net after a good, deep serve, or an approach shot. Aim to play your volley low and deep to the baseline, or at an angle out of your opponent's reach.

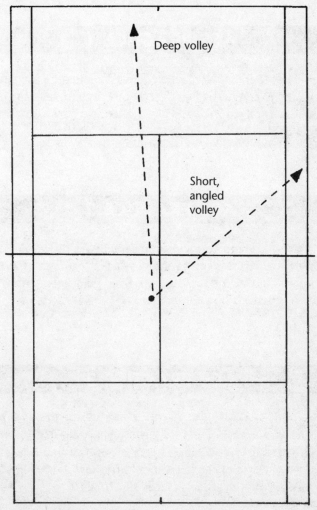

Deep volley

Short, angled volley

Practising volleys

The three main things to focus on when you're practising volleys are:

1 punching your racket crisply at the ball
2 keeping your wrist firm
3 directing the ball away from your opponent

ACE PRACTICE 1

To practise the punching action, chalk a circle on a wall and stand about 2 m away. Practise stepping in and volleying balls at it. Try five forehand volleys, then five backhand volleys to start with.

ACE PRACTICE 2

To practise keeping your wrist firm, hold your racket out in front of you. Ask a friend to throw a ball at your racket, fast and from close range (be careful!). Keep your wrist firm as the ball rebounds off your racket.

ACE PRACTICE 3

To improve your placement, ask a friend (Player B) to feed balls to your forehand and backhand volleys alternately. Move in to punch the ball deep, then return to the centre service line for the next volley. Put targets down to help you aim deep and at short angles (see next page).

Ace Practice 3

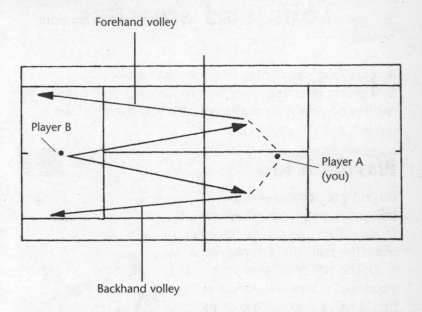

Forehand volley

Player B

Player A
(you)

Backhand volley

Coach tips

- Don't swing your racket at the ball,
  but punch the ball out in front of you,
  using your shoulder as a hinge. Your
  arm and shoulder muscles shouldn't
  be too stiff.
- Keep your racket head up above your hand.
- Keep the take-back and follow-through short.
- If you find volleying difficult at first, try moving your hand
  further up the racket handle to give you more control.
- Use both arms to volley. Imagine your non-hitting arm
  leaning on a work surface as you turn your shoulder in
  towards the ball.

6 Lobs and smashes

Now that you've mastered the basic strokes, it's time to get more ambitious. Ready to spice up your game with two brand-new weapons? Good, it's that dynamic duo – the lob and the smash.

Playing a lob

Playing the occasional lob is a brilliant way of catching opponents off guard. But be careful how you place the ball. The aim of a lob is to hit the ball high, over your opponent's head. Too low, and they'll be able to reach it easily, too high, and they'll have time to run back and wait for it to bounce. Ideally, aim the ball a few centimetres above your opponent's outstretched racket.

GETTING TO GRIPS

You can play lobs on the forehand and backhand sides. Use your normal groundstroke grip.

Forehand grip

Backhand grip

The forehand lob

1 From the ready position, shape up as you would for a forehand drive. Turn sideways on your right foot and take your racket back.

2 Start stepping in with your left foot, swinging your racket in a steep low-to-high action to lift the ball high into the air.

3 Aim to hit the ball slightly out in front of you, about an arm's length from your body. Use your non-hitting arm for balance.

4 Follow through high, in the direction of the ball. Your racket should finish high above your head.

The backhand lob

Use the same technique to play a backhand lob. Shape up for the shot as you would for a backhand drive. Don't panic if you find this a trickier shot to play – just keep practising!

Lob tactics

You can use the lob for both attack and defence. Use it to attack an opponent at the net and break up their pattern of play. Use it for defence if your opponent has forced you back or out wide – this gives you time to recover for your next shot. Aim your lob deep over your opponent's backhand side.

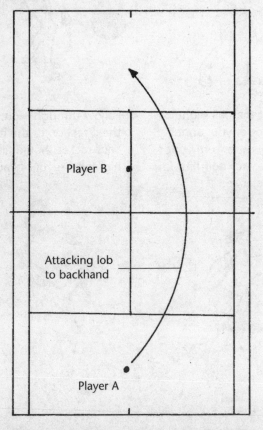

Player B

Attacking lob
to backhand

Player A

Coach tips

- Use the same basic action as for your groundstrokes, swinging your racket through the ball.
- Keep your racket face 'open' (angled upwards) to lift the ball into the air.
- Don't snatch at the ball. Keep the swing smooth, slow and under control.
- Attacking lobs are best played with topspin. This makes the ball bounce high and kick away.
- Fool your opponent into thinking that you're shaping up to play a groundstroke, then play a lob.

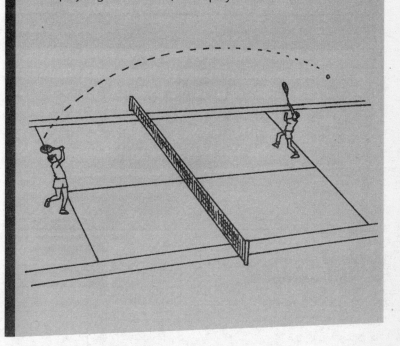

Playing a smash

The most dramatic way to
counter a lob is to smash the ball
away for a winner. A smash is hit
from high to low before the ball
has bounced and uses a similar
throwing action to the serve.
Played well, the smash can be
one of the most exciting
shots in tennis, winning you

points outright and leaving opponents stranded. But be
careful – it's also one of the easiest shots to mess up!

GETTING TO GRIPS

Use the 'chopper' or service grip
to hit your smashes. You can start
off using your groundstroke grips
to build up your confidence. But
make sure you switch to the
'chopper' grip.

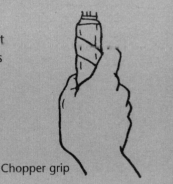

Chopper grip

HOT SHOTS

Pete Sampras regularly thrills crowds with his spectacular
jump smash, nicknamed the 'slam dunk' from the basketball
shot. This is a very tricky shot to play, needing strength,
perfect footwork and rock-solid racket control. Sampras
never takes his eyes off the ball, even when he's a metre
off the ground. If you can pull this shot off, you're on to
a winner!

The forehand smash

1 From the ready position, turn on your right foot and move sideways and backwards as soon as your opponent hits the lob.

2 Take your racket back and up, keeping your eyes on the ball. Point at the ball with your free hand to help you focus as you hit.

3 Aim to hit the ball at full stretch. Throw your racket at the ball and put your weight into the shot for power.

4 Follow through in the direction of the ball, so your racket finishes down by your left-hand side. Quickly get back into position for the next shot.

The backhand smash

You play the backhand smash in a similar way to the forehand. Don't worry if it doesn't come easily – it's actually one of the trickiest shots to play. If you're not feeling confident, run back to the baseline, let the ball bounce and play an ordinary backhand or forehand. Or run around the ball and hit a forehand smash.

Coach tips

- Throw your racket at the ball as you would for a serve. Throw the racket up and out at the ball.
- Your arms should work like a bow and arrow. Pull your racket back behind your head as if you are pulling the bow back ready to shoot the arrow.
- Good footwork is crucial. Get into position quickly with a mixture of side steps and skips, rather than running. Move sideways and backwards.
- Get into position by beating the ball backwards. Your head should be under the ball as you hit.

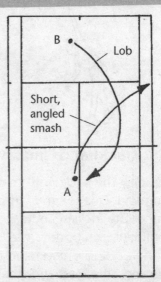

- Don't try to whack the ball as hard as possible. Concentrate on your aim, timing and on watching the ball!

Smash tactics

Use the smash to counter your opponent's lob, which may be when you've come to the net ready to play an attacking volley. Hit the smash to your opponent's weaker side, either deep into the far corners or at a wide angle.

B

Lob

Short, angled smash

A

Facing a smash

So what can you do if the tables
are turned and you end up being
smashed at? Do you stand any
chance of getting the ball back?
If the smash is hit well, the
answer is probably no! But don't
give up without a fight – try to
anticipate where your opponent
is aiming the ball, then get
back behind the baseline. It's
possible that you might just be
able to get your racket to the
ball and block it back.

ACE PRACTICE

The best way to improve your lobs and smashes is to
practise the two shots together with a friend. One of you
(Player A) should stand on the baseline and throw up lobs.
The other (Player B) should stand on the centre service line,
about 2 m from the net, and return them with smashes.
Try this five times and then change over.

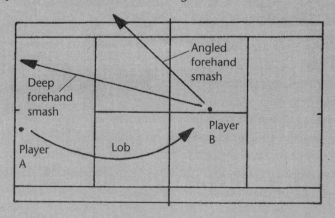

Angled
forehand
smash

Deep
forehand
smash

Player
B

Player
A

Lob

7 In a spin

Adding variety

When you're playing a match, you need to keep opponents guessing about your next move. If your shots and tactics become too predictable, they'll always be ready with a reply. Catch them off balance and off guard by playing some shots with spin. There are two main types – topspin and slice (or backspin).

Use topspin for:

- Better ball control
- Making the ball kick through on the bounce
- Dipping the ball at a volleyer's feet
- Looping the ball high into the air and for slowing play down

Use slice for:

- Making the ball skid low or getting it to stop
- Playing the ball lower over the net
- Making it harder for an opponent to use topspin
- Changing the pace of the game by slowing the rate of play down

Putting a spin on it

Putting spin on the ball changes the way the ball flies through the air and the way it bounces when it hits the ground. To make the ball spin, you need to alter the angle of your racket face as you hit the ball. Read on to find out how to hit the ball flat, with topspin and with slice, and how the ball behaves.

Flat stroke

Racket face: the racket face is at right angles to the ground so that it hits the ball squarely.
Flight of ball: the ball flies off the racket straight ahead before gravity makes it dip down.
Ball bounce: the ball bounces evenly at about the same angle as it hits the ground.

Topspin stroke

Racket face: the racket face is 'closed' to play the ball down and make it spin forwards. Stroke the racket up and over the back of the ball.
Flight of ball: the ball travels higher over the net and dips steeply at the end of its flight.
Ball bounce: the ball bounces sharply upwards and forwards, kicking away from your opponent's feet.

Sliced stroke

Racket face: the racket face is 'open' to play the ball upwards and make it spin backwards. Stroke the racket down and under the back of the ball.
Flight of ball: the ball floats low over the net and stays in the air longer.
Ball bounce: slice deadens the bounce so the ball bounces low and may skid at your opponent's feet.

Spin and slice

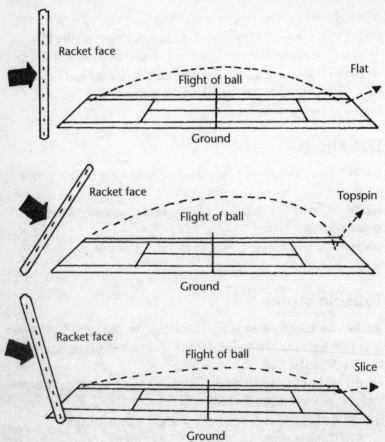

Racket face

Flight of ball

Flat

Ground

Racket face

Flight of ball

Topspin

Ground

Racket face

Flight of ball

Slice

Ground

Countering spin

What if your opponent uses spin against you? Now it's your turn to read the flight and bounce of the ball and judge how it will behave. A general rule is to use topspin to counter slice, and slice to counter topspin.

Topspin forehand

Hitting your forehand with topspin lets you strike the ball harder and still enables you to land it in court. The ball travels higher over the net, with a greater margin of error.

1 From the ready position, prepare as you would for a normal forehand, but take your racket back below the height of the on-coming ball.

2 Swing the racket upwards from low to high, brushing up and over the back of the ball.

3 Follow through high so that your racket head finishes behind your left shoulder.

GETTING TO GRIPS

Use your normal eastern forehand grip to play topspin forehands. Some players like to get extra topspin by moving their hand further round to the right of the racket handle to give a semi-western grip.

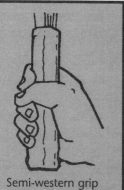

Semi-western grip

Sliced backhand

A sliced backhand, hit deep, is an excellent defensive shot.
Use your normal backhand grip.

1 From the ready position,
   prepare as you would for
   a normal backhand, but
   keep your backswing
   short and take your
   racket back high.

2 Swing the racket
   down and through
   the ball, slicing from
   high to low behind
   and under the ball.
   It should feel as if
   you are holding the
   ball slightly longer
   on your strings than
   for a normal drive.

3 Follow through in
   the direction of the
   ball, keeping your racket
   face open to maximise
   the slice.

Approach shot

*Use your sliced backhands as 'approach shots' to give you
time to get to the net. You need to pick the right time to
play an approach shot, for example when your opponent
has hit a short ball. That is the time to attack!*

Spinning serves

Most players have a variety of serves which they use to exploit opponents' weaknesses or take them by surprise. Adding spin and slice is also useful for second serves where security is vital. Use your normal 'chopper' grip.

Topspin serve

Adding topspin makes the ball loop high over the net, which is great news for a second serve. The ball also kicks forward as it lands making it tricky to return. Toss the ball up slightly further to your left than usual and brush your racket up and over the back of the ball.

Sliced serve

Slicing the serve makes it swerve sideways, forcing your opponent to stretch. Toss the ball up slightly further to your right than usual. Hit down and under the ball, slicing from right to left (for right-handers).

Touch shots

Instead of blasting out groundstrokes all the time, mix things up with a drop shot. This is an example of a 'touch' shot, a delicate shot played with slice. Use your usual forehand and backhand grips.

The forehand drop shot

1 From the ready position, shape up as if you were going to play a forehand drive shot.

2 Step in with your left leg and swing your racket at the ball.

3 Brush the racket face down and under the ball, bringing the racket right underneath the ball to slice it.

4 Follow through in the direction of the ball to maximise the slice.

Backhand drop shot

Use the same technique to play a backhand drop shot. You might find this easier because it feels more natural to slice the ball across your body. Double-handers should try using one hand only on this delicate stroke.

Drop volley

Drop shots are played like
groundstrokes, often from
mid-court, after the ball has
bounced. Drop volleys are
very similar except that
they're played at the net
before the bounce. Use your
usual volleying grip and
shape up as you would to
play a normal volley with a
short backswing. Play the
ball with an open racket face
to increase the slice, taking the
pace off the ball as it drops over the net.

Touch shot tactics

Use drop shots to catch your opponent out of position.
They're brilliant for breaking up baseline rallies, forcing
opponents to race to the net. Even if they can reach the
ball, they may only be able to play a weak reply, giving you
a chance to play a lob or passing shot. It is a great tactic to
use against slow movers!

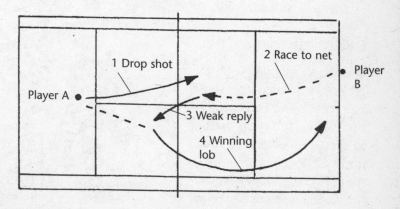

1 Drop shot

2 Race to net

Player A

Player B

3 Weak reply

4 Winning lob

Coach tips

- Dropshots are ideal for clay or grass courts. On a slow surface like clay, the ball keeps low and on faster grass, it skids away. It's trickier to play a good drop shot on a hard court as the higher bounce gives opponents more time to reach the ball.

- For drop shots and volleys, take your racket back higher than normal. Then bend your knees to get right down to the ball.

- Try to make the ball bounce as close to the other side of the net as possible.

- Slice down and under the ball as if you are turning a key in a lock.

- You need 'soft hands' to play touch shots, which means excellent racket skills, based on delicate control rather than power.

ACE PRACTICE

Practise drop shots by placing two buckets about a metre or so on the other side of the net. Get a friend (Player B) to feed balls to you and aim to land the ball in the buckets. Move the buckets out into the tramlines to practise angled drop shots.

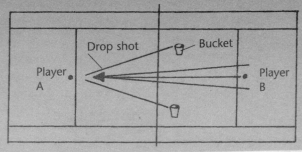

Master of disguise

A tennis match is like a game of chess – you always have to keep your opponent guessing about your next move. Creating a combination of powerful groundstrokes, sharp volleys, and touch shots is a good start and for added surprise, try disguising your drop shots as something else. Shape up as you would to play a groundstroke, taking the racket back early and turning side on. Then, at the last moment, slow your swing right down and play a delicate drop shot instead.

HOT SHOTS

Sisters Venus and Serena Williams (USA) play a power game, hitting the ball with incredible pace and accuracy. But they also have great touch and can fool opponents into expecting another cracking drive, then popping a drop shot over the net.

Grand Slam

Wimbledon

When held: June/July
Where held: All England Lawn Tennis Club, Wimbledon, London
Playing surface: Grass

Summer wouldn't be summer without Wimbledon. The last major tournament to be played on grass, Wimbledon is famous for its traditions – the royal box, the strawberries and cream, the queue for tickets and the rain stopping play. Each year, the world's top players meet at Wimbledon to battle it out for the most coveted title in tennis.

The first Wimbledon championships were held in 1877 when the only event was the men's singles, won by British player, Spencer Gore. Two hundred spectators paid a shilling to watch (compared to the 15,000 who watch the final today). The ladies' singles was added in 1884 and was first won by Maud Watson.

Playing on grass means that Wimbledon is ideally suited to the big serve-and-volleyers. But baseliners have also made their mark – Chris Evert, Jimmy Connors and Andre Agassi to name just a few. It's also the place for a big fashion statement, being the only major tournament where players must still dress in 'almost entirely white' clothes.

Championship points

- At the 1999 Championships, 36,000 balls were used and 27,000 kg of strawberries and 7,000 litres of cream were eaten.

- Billie-Jean King of the USA holds the all-time record for Wimbledon titles, with 19 titles in singles and doubles. Martina Navratilova has a record nine singles titles. In the men's game, Bjorn Borg famously won the title five times in a row. Pete Sampras has won six times in seven years, so far...

- In 1985, Germany's Boris Becker became the youngest player (at 17 years and 227 days) and the first unseeded player to win the men's singles. In 1996, Martina Hingis become the youngest ever champion, winning the Ladies' Doubles, aged 15 years and 282 days.

8 Playing a match

You've polished all your shots and put in hours of practice and now the moment you've been waiting for has finally come. It's match day! Feeling nervous? Don't panic. Try to relax and enjoy yourself, even if things don't go according to plan.

Match preparation

Here are some tips as you prepare for match play:

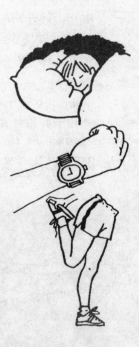

- Get a good night's sleep.
- Eat a good meal at least two hours before you play, with lots of energy-packed food like pasta and drink plenty of fluids.
- Pack your tennis bag.
- Arrive in good time – you'll be hot and bothered if you're late.
- Do your stretches and warm-up exercises (see pages 112–115).
- Make sure you get a proper pre-match knock-up with your opponent (see pages 81 and 82).

Pre-match practice

Try to fit in a warm-up session before the match with your coach or a friend. Practise all your shots so that you go on court feeling confident in your game. Hit for about 15 to 20 minutes about an hour before play begins. But don't overdo things!

What to take on court

Take time to pack your tennis bag calmly before a match and make sure you've got everything you'll need on court. Consult the following checklist before going on court.

Equipment checklist

- Racket (and a spare in case you break a string)
- Can of balls
- Sweatshirt or tracksuit
- Fresh shirt or set of clothes (in case you get very sweaty)
- Extra pair of socks
- Headband or hairband
- Wristbands
- Towel
- Baseball cap or visor (in case it's sunny)
- Sunglasses
- Sunscreen (if it's going to be hot)
- Water bottle
- Bananas and/
  or a high-energy bar

Waiting around

All players have different ways of passing the time when waiting to go on court. Some sit quietly by themselves, reading a book or listening to CDs. Others prefer to have company. They might play cards or talk over their strategy with their coach or friends. Above all, try to stay relaxed!

Having a game plan

Tennis isn't all about having good shots. To win a match, you need to work out a game plan before you go on court.

Getting to know your opponent

Find out as much as possible about your opponent so that you can work out the best tactics to use. Apart from playing against them, top players also watch videos of opponents' matches to build up a fuller picture. Here are some of the key questions you need to ask:

- What are your opponent's strengths? Is he or she better on the forehand or backhand?
- What are your opponent's weaknesses? Does he or she have problems reaching up for overheads, for example?
- Is your opponent quick on court? Or are they slow on their feet and reluctant to run?
- Is your opponent left- or right-handed? You'll need to adjust your tactics accordingly.
- Is your opponent easygoing or easily ruffled? They may lose concentration if things don't go their way.

Getting to know your own game

You also need to analyse your own game so that you can base your tactics on exploiting your strengths and covering up your weaknesses. Here are some questions to ask yourself:

- What are your strengths? Try to play your favourite shots to your opponent's weaknesses.
- What are your weaknesses? You'll still need to play these shots, so make sure you practise them beforehand.
- What type of player are you – do you prefer to rally from the baseline or go into the net to volley?
- Are you fighting fit? This will let you cover more of the court and play more attacking tennis.

Your game plan

Now put the two sets of answers together and base your game plan on them. For example, if your opponent has a weak backhand, attack it with your favourite forehand. If your opponent hates to volley, play a drop shot to force them into the net. Jot your game plan down so you can look at it during the match.

Shot selection

To win a tennis match, you need to select the right shot to play at the right time. If you don't pick the right moment to use them, you'll make needless errors. Here are a few pointers to bear in mind:

- Attack short balls
- Play deep balls defensively
- Play low-bouncing balls defensively
- Attack balls which bounce between waist and shoulder height

ACE PRACTICE

Before a match, practise playing points in your head and try to visualise what your strokes should look like. Imagine hitting a perfect forehand, or serving for the Wimbledon final.

HOT SHOTS

Among her many other achievements, Martina Hingis (Switzerland) won Wimbledon when she was just 15 years old, the youngest ever to do so. Named after the all-time great, Martina Navratilova, Hingis is a brilliant match player, able to select exactly the right shot at the right time.

Knock, knock

Once you've arrived on court, and tossed for ends, you're ready to start the knock-up. In top tournaments, the rules allow players to knock up for five minutes before play begins. This is a time for players to practise their shots and to get used to the court surface. There's no set form for the knock-up but players usually practise groundstrokes, volleys, lobs and smashes, serves and returns in that order.

Using the knock-up

Even if you're only playing a friendly match, you can still put the knock-up to good use. It's your last, big chance to...

• Try out your shots
• Think about your game plan
• Analyse your own game
• Assess your opponent's game

Coach tips

- Make sure you practise all of your shots in the knock-up.
- You should try to return some of your opponent's serves.
- Don't go for winning shots, but concentrate on accuracy and keeping the ball in play.
- Practising lobs and throwing up the ball to serve will help you check which way the wind is blowing and where the sun is (if you're playing outdoors).
- Try moving your opponent about a bit to see how well he or she moves around the court.
- Note if your opponent hits with lots of topspin or slice and how they react when you do the same.

Coping with nerves

Got butterflies in your stomach? Feel like turning round and running away? Don't worry! Feeling nervous before a big match is perfectly normal and some stress is good for getting the adrenaline flowing and getting you pumped up to play. However, too much stress can stop you playing at your best. Take a few deep breaths to help you relax, and concentrate on playing one point at a time. For more about mental attitude, see chapter 10.

Unforced errors

Picture the scene... you're 4-1 up in the final set and you think you're cruising. Then your mind starts to wander. Before you know it, a couple of your shots land into the net, a couple land out and you serve a handful of double faults. Your opponent breaks back and goes on to win the match.

You're not alone! Losing concentration is the easiest thing in the world to do. But this is when unforced errors creep in, and many matches are lost by one player making more unforced errors than the other. Don't let it happen to you!

Percentage tennis

'Playing the percentage' means going for more basic shots which have a higher percentage of going in, rather than trying to hit harder, riskier winners. Keep the ball in play and wait for your opponent to make the first mistake.

Minding your manners

Tennis can be a really frustrating game and during a match it can be difficult to keep your cool if things start to go wrong. But minding your manners is a must. Here's a ten-point guide to tennis etiquette:

1. If you're calling your own lines, try to be fair.
2. Never argue over a line call, even if you think it is wrong. Agree on a let and play the point again.
3. If you think opponents are making bad calls on purpose, stay calm. Ask them if they're sure, then get on with the game or ask for a let.
4. Only call balls on your side of the net. Balls on the other side are your opponent's call.
5. Never shout, scream or swear at your opponent.
6. Never slam your racket down on the ground or hit stray balls in anger.
7. Win or lose, shake hands with your opponent after the match and thank them for the game.
8. Never argue with the umpire. They have the power to penalise you for bad behaviour.
9. Don't forget, bad behaviour can easily backfire and end up putting you off.
10. In any event, your best option is to beat your opponent by your sheer skill and brilliance!

Don't make excuses

It seems really obvious but half of all players involved in
tennis matches will lose. You should never be frightened
of losing – it's always a possibility. Try to accept defeat
graciously and learn from your mistakes. Don't give up, feel
sorry for yourself or make excuses. You've probably lost
because your opponent played better and not because you
were feeling tired, or your shoulder hurt, or you couldn't
see because of the sun!

Enjoy yourself

If you enjoy playing matches, you're far more likely to end
up a winner than if you loathe and dread them. Try to look
forward to the challenge. That way, you'll probably find it
easier to relax and keep any nerves under control. Besides,
what's the point of doing something if you're not going to
enjoy it?

9 Match tactics

Once you've analysed your opponent's game, you'll need to work out the best tactics to use. In this chapter, you'll find out about some of the different tactics for playing singles and doubles. Then it's a case of getting out there and putting everything you've learnt into action!

The five basics

There are five basic tactics you should always base your game on. You can find out more about them later on in this chapter.

1 Know where to stand
2 Put and keep the ball in play
3 Make your opponent move
4 Play on your opponent's weaknesses
5 Wrong-foot your opponent

Coach tips

- Don't be tempted to overhit, particularly on the big points, such as deuce, advantage, game and set points. Instead, hit the ball at three-quarter pace.
- Don't try to hit the lines all the time. Aim just inside the lines to lessen the risk of the ball landing out.
- If in doubt about which shot to use, choose your most reliable shot. Hit all your shots with a purpose.
- Keep opponents guessing by making them think you are going to their weaker side, then changing direction.
- Use drop shots and lobs to mix things up a bit and upset your opponent's rhythm.
- It's safer to hit shots cross-court over the lower part of the net than down the lines.
- Move your opponent from side to side by playing the ball into the gaps.
- Play one shot at a time. Try not to think ahead to when you've won (or lost) the next point, game or set. Concentrate on the point in hand.
- Keep calm and try to think about your game plan between points.

Serving for the match

Whether you're playing singles or doubles, knowing where to stand on court is essential for getting into the right position to hit the ball.

Serving in singles

In singles, stand about 30 cm to the left or right of the centre mark, as close to the baseline as possible (but watch out for foot faults!). From this central position, you'll be able to run into the net to volley, or move easily to either side to cover the return.

Serving in doubles

In doubles, stand halfway between the centre mark and the doubles' sideline. This will allow you to cover your side of the court and reach cross-court shots into the tramlines. You will also be able to reach shots down the centre of the court, and will be in a good position for quickly running into the net to volley.

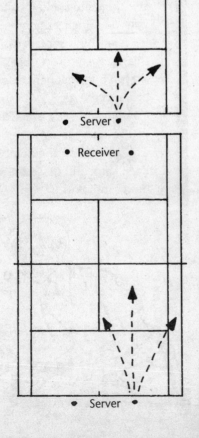

Serve tactics

In both singles and doubles, take advantage of your opponent's weakness by serving to that side, for example if he or she has a weaker backhand. However, do not do this every time – slip in the occasional serve to the forehand side to keep your opponent guessing.

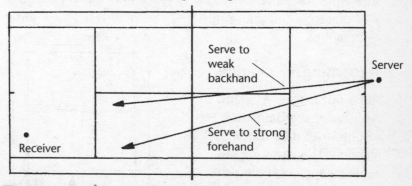

Coach tips

- Vary your serve by moving out towards the sidelines to slice at an angle to the deuce (right) court or hit a topspin serve wide to the advantage (left) side of the court.

- If you're having problems with your serve going long, try standing a few centimetres further back behind the baseline.

- Get your first serve in, particularly on the big points, such as deuce, advantage, game and set points.

- Serving down the centre in doubles cuts down the angles for the return and gives your partner a better chance of intercepting and responding with a powerful shot.

- Don't be rushed into serving before you are ready. Bouncing the ball a few times before serving will help you concentrate and steady yourself.

Returning serve

To win a match, you'll need to win at least one of your
opponent's service games in each set (or a service point in
a tie-break). This is called 'breaking' the serve. So returning
well is just as important as good serving. Where you stand
and what sort of return you play really depends on the pace
and placement of your opponent's serve. But here are some
general tips.

Returning in singles

For a fast first serve, stand
on or near the baseline
about 1 m inside the singles'
sideline. This gives you an
equal chance of hitting the
return with your forehand
or backhand. Against a
weaker server, move inside
the baseline ready to move
in and attack a short ball.

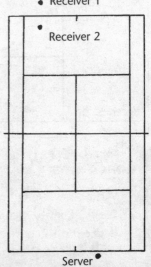

Returning in doubles

In doubles, stand halfway between the centre mark and the
doubles' sidelines. This will allow you to move to either side
to return a wide serve to the corner, or down the centre
service line.

HOT SHOTS

Andre Agassi (USA) is one of the best returners of serve in the
game. He plays the ball early on the rise (this means before
it reaches the top of the bounce) and drives it back with
enormous power, giving the server very little time to react.

Varying your return

Depending on how fast your opponent serves, you may have to adapt your normal groundstroke returns. Here are two options:

- Blocked return – punch your racket at the ball, to return a fast, deep serve.
- Chipped return – hit the ball firmly with slice, to return high, topspin serves.

Coach tips

- If you're facing a big server, stand about 1 m behind the baseline to give you more time to play the ball.
- Get back to the middle of the baseline after hitting the ball so you can cover both sides of the court.
- If you hit a chipped return, move into the net to volley. This tactic is called 'chip and charge'.
- Try to guess where your opponent is likely to serve so that you can move into position quickly. It can sometimes be tricky, but try to 'read' the flight of the ball from the moment it leaves your opponent's racket.

Singles tactics

Playing singles is all about stamina and concentration. With the whole court to cover, you'll need to be fit to stay in the game and keep long, hard rallies going.

Baseline play

Some players like to use their strong groundstrokes to build rallies from the baseline. The aim is to keep the ball in play until you spot the chance to play a winner, or force your opponent into making a mistake.

Going for the gaps

Hit the ball first to one side of the court, then the other to move opponents from side to side. Aim your shots into the gaps. This will test your opponents' stamina and force them to play difficult shots on the run.

Wrong footing

Catch opponents out by 'wrong-footing' them. Hit the ball first to one side, then the other (as above). Then suddenly hit the ball to the same side twice running. If your opponent has already started to run to cover the gap, you'll catch him or her on the wrong foot.

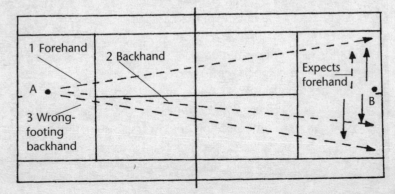

Serve and volley

On fast surfaces such as grass, try to volley after your serve. In this attacking type of play, you hit a good first serve then follow it in to the net to volley.

How to serve and volley

1 Throw the ball up to serve, slightly further in front of you than normal.

2 Play a good, deep serve, starting to move into the court as you follow through.

3 As your opponent returns the ball, 'split step' to play your first volley deep into the corner of the court. Read on to find how to split step.

4 Keep moving in towards the net and split step again for your second, winning volley.

Split stepping

To split step, simply land with your feet shoulder-width apart and your knees slightly bent. Do this as your opponent plays the ball. It will help you to balance so you are ready to spring to either side to play the volley.

Coach tips

- Taking up a position at the net is intimidating for an opponent and makes it more difficult for them to pass you.

- Even if you're a natural baseliner, surprise your opponent by sometimes following your serve into the net.

- Once you decide to go, go! Don't hesitate and get caught with the on-coming ball at your feet.

- Serve down the middle to make it more difficult for your opponent to hit a cross-court return which you have to stretch to reach.

Doubles tactics

All the points about strokeplay and concentration also apply to playing doubles, with one important extra! Playing doubles is all about team work. You're no longer out there on your own, making all your own decisions. Now you've got a partner to worry about, too!

Where to stand

For doubles, the tramlines come into use to give a bigger court area. As a general rule, each player covers half of their end of the court. It's vitally important that you choose your starting positions carefully, to make sure you can cover your half easily and can run quickly into the net to volley. After the first point, the server and their partner change sides. The receiver moves forwards and their partner moves back in order to return the serve.

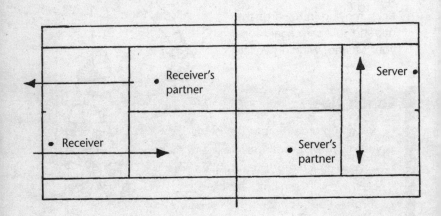

Changing places

You sometimes
see players
altering their
starting positions
against opponents
with a particularly
strong shot, such
as a cross-court
return. SP moves
across to stand on
the same side as
S. S stands close
to the centre
mark to serve so
that he or she can
move quickly
across to cover
the empty court.
When R plays
the cross-court,
SP is in a good
position to volley
it away. This is
called the
Australian or
'I' formation.

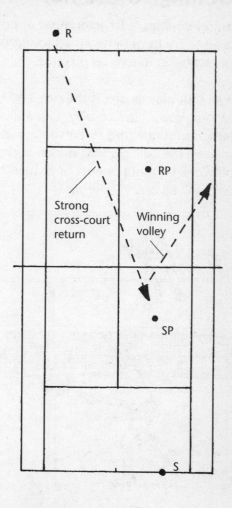

Strong
cross-court
return

Winning
volley

Key:
S = Server
SP = Server's partner
R = Receiver
RP = Receiver's partner

Getting to the net

In top doubles, a large number of points are won by volleys. Try to get into an attacking position at the net as often and as quickly as possible.

If all four players are at the net, and the action is fast and furious, you'll have to play your volleys by instinct. Good basic techniques are essential for these 'reflex' volleys. Try to keep the ball low and punch your volleys downwards, between your opponents or at their feet. Any high or weak balls will be quickly put away.

Picking on someone

A good tactic in doubles is to play the ball at the weaker player in the opposite pair. Putting him or her under pressure may lead to mistakes and, in turn, to a loss of confidence. But be prepared to change your tactics if this player starts to read and hit the ball very well.

Teamwork

Working with your partner as a team is the key to good doubles. The best doubles teams have great on-court understanding. They know each other's strengths and weaknesses, encourage each other and move together around the court. Agree your strategy before the match, and never blame your partner if things go wrong!

Finding a partner

If you prefer playing in the right court, chose someone who's comfortable in the left. Ideally, the right-court player should have a strong cross-court return and a good backhand volley. The left-court player should be able to play good returns off the backhand and have a strong forehand volley. Many of the most successful doubles partnerships have one left-handed and one right-handed player. You should also both be happy to go to the net.

Moving together

Staying alert as your partner plays the ball is vital in doubles as you must be ready to cover the rest of the court and play the shot if your partner misses. You should try to move into the net together, and, if one of you runs back for a lob, the other should go too.

Good communication

Being part of a team, it's essential that you communicate with your partner so that you both know what to do and where to move. It'll also spare you the embarrassment of both going for the same ball, or both leaving it to the other! Work out a system of simple one-word calls.

Coach tips

- Hit the ball down the middle of the court, between your opponents, to cause confusion.
- If this happens to you, the ball should be played by whoever can reach it with a forehand.
- When returning serve, keep the net player guessing by occasionally going down his or her line, rather than cross court.
- Don't be afraid to intercept, or 'poach' if you're at the net – move across and intercept cross-court shots with a volley. But don't change your mind halfway through, and don't move too early or your opponent will pass you down the tramline.
- Confuse opponents by moving slightly as if you mean to intercept, then moving back again so that your partner can play the shot.

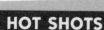

HOT SHOTS

The most successful doubles team of modern times was Martina Navratilova (a left-hander) and Pam Shriver (a right-hander). In their 10-year partnership, the pair won an astonishing 79 titles, including 20 Grand Slams (7 Australian Opens, 5 Wimbledons, 4 French Opens and 4 US Opens).

Adapting your game

If you're used to playing on grass, having to switch to play a match on clay can be an uncomfortable experience. Different court surfaces change the way the ball bounces, giving you more or less time to play your shots, so you need to be able to adapt your game to suit the playing conditions. Get as much experience as you can on different surfaces.

Fast and slow

- On 'fast' courts, the ball bounces fast and low, and skids through after bouncing. You'll have less time to play the ball, so make your backswing shorter on your groundstrokes. The best tactic to use on fast surfaces is serve and volley, where you can 'kill' the ball. Fast courts are grass, cement and indoor carpet.
- On 'slow' courts, the ball bounces more slowly and higher off the ground, meaning that you'll have more time to prepare for shots. Be ready to rally from the baseline with more topspin. Slow courts are clay, shale and all-weather surfaces like tarmac.

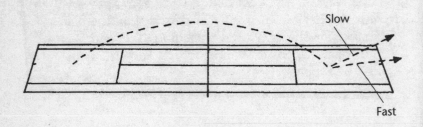

Slow

Fast

Playing indoors

There may be no sun or wind to disrupt play indoors, but there can be other drawbacks. Lights can be either too bright or too dim, and it might get very hot so have plenty to drink. Also, carpet courts grip your shoes, so wear special smooth soles or an old, slightly worn pair of shoes.

Coach tips for difficult weather

- If you're serving into the sun, get your first serve in by serving slightly more slowly and carefully.
- Let high lobs bounce so you're not staring into the sun.
- Playing into the wind will slow your shots down. Hit the ball higher over the net and aim deeper than normal.
- If the wind is behind you, your shots will fly faster through the air. Hit the ball lower over the net and use topspin to keep the ball in.
- Don't aim your shots as deep as usual – the wind may blow them out.

Improving your game

Even the best players are always looking to improve their game. The first step is to spot mistakes and then put them right, taking each shot in turn. Ask yourself questions about what's going wrong and then work on the solutions.

? **Problem:** My serve keeps going out.

✓ **Solution:** Take the pace off and concentrate on getting the ball in.

? **Problem:** No matter how hard I try, my groundstrokes keep going into the net.

✓ **Solution:** Hit the ball higher over the net, keeping your wrist firm, and your racket face up.

? **Problem:** I keep hitting volleys out of court.

✓ **Solution:** Punch your racket face, not your hand, at the ball. Point your racket face towards the target.

? **Problem:** I can't hit lobs high enough.

✓ **Solution:** Swing more from low to high, with a long follow-through. Keep your racket face open.

? **Problem:** I keep missing the ball when I smash.

✓ **Solution:** Watch the ball, not the target. Don't try to hit the ball too hard, but concentrate on placement instead.

Having an off day

Everyone has an off day on court. Do you pack up and go home? No way! Read on for some tips on turning things around.

Coach tips

- Go back to basics – work on racket control, footwork, and early preparation.
- Keep calm – losing your temper will help you lose the match.
- Take your time between points, especially on serve.
- Don't try to do too much with the ball. Hit cross court or down the centre of the court, over the lowest part of the net.
- Play percentage tennis (see page 83).
- And finally, watch the ball! Your concentration and consistency will soon improve.

Team tennis:
The Davis Cup

In team tennis, the biggest competition for men is the Davis Cup. First held in 1900, between the USA and Great Britain, the Davis Cup has gone from strength to strength. Today, more than 70 countries take part. Teams are divided or 'zoned' geographically and competition is fierce to gain entry into the elite World Group, the Davis Cup's top division. Here 16 nations battle it out for the honour of reaching the final.

The competition was the brainwave of American Dwight Davis who donated the cup and played in the very first match which took place at the Longwood Cricket Club in Boston, USA. Davis was captain of the victorious USA team.

Championship points

- *Apart from the USA and Great Britain, no other countries took part until 1904 when France and Belgium joined.*

- *The first British Davis Cup team had a very casual approach to practising. They went sightseeing at Niagara Falls instead!*

- *From 1900-1971, the Davis Cup used a Challenge Round format. This meant that the previous year's holders sat it out and waited to be challenged by the present year's winners.*

Tennis at the Olympics

Tennis was reintroduced as a full Olympic sport at the 1988 Seoul Games. (Previously, it was last played in the Olympics in 1924.) Steffi Graf completed a unique 'Golden Slam' by adding the women's singles title to her Grand Slam of Grand Slams. Miloslav Mecir won the men's singles gold for Czechoslovakia. Wheelchair players take part in the Paralympics after the main Games.

10 Fit for tennis?

Playing tennis isn't all about good technique. To play and win, you need to be physically fit and mentally tough. The great American player, Jimmy Connors, said that tennis was 95% in the mind, and he had one of the toughest minds around.

Focus and concentration

Concentrate on playing your shots and sticking to your game plan. Don't let yourself get distracted, especially if you're winning. Learn to give 100% effort even in practice so that you take this attitude with you on to the court. It's often the most determined player who comes out the winner.

Positive thinking

Train yourself to think like a winner. There's no point going on court believing that you're going to lose, because you will! Don't think back over lost points or opportunities – it'll only discourage you. Think positive, encouraging thoughts and smile if you make a mistake. It'll cheer you up and it will also confuse your opponent!

Feeling confident

Confidence comes from playing well, so it can be a vicious circle. If you're having a bad day, you'll lose confidence, and if you lose confidence, you'll probably play badly. Playing well is the key to growing in confidence. And the way to do that is...to practise!

Body language

Look confident and you'll feel confident. Walk tall, with your shoulders back and a determined look on your face. If you look like a winner, you'll play like a winner.

Fit for tennis?

Keeping your cool

Never get angry with yourself – if you want to win, you'll need to keep a cool head. Very few players are good enough to lose their temper and still go on to win, although John McEnroe is an exception! Tennis can be frustrating, but losing concentration will only help you lose the match.

Staying relaxed

Try to stay relaxed on court, but don't try too hard as you'll probably end up feeling more tense! If you start feeling anxious, your muscles will start tightening up and too much tension can cause players to 'choke'. This means you get so tight that you miss one shot, then another... So think positively and stay loose!

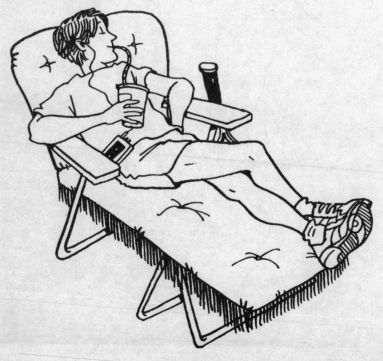

Coach tips

- If you're getting tight, slow your movement and breathing down.
- Some players 'grunt' as they hit the ball. What they're actually doing is breathing out noisily to help relax their muscles. So it's not just for effect!
- To stay focused between points, look down at your racket or adjust the strings so your mind doesn't wander.
- If a call goes against you, accept it and get on with the rest of the game. Don't keep brooding about it.
- Play one point at a time and don't dwell on past mistakes.
- Don't let yourself get scared by your opponent's reputation. Forget who they are and concentrate on playing your shots.
- Don't lose concentration if you're ahead. You still need to win the last few points.
- Above all, believe in yourself – you can do it! And if you do get beaten, remember that it's not the end of the world. Put it all down to experience.

ACE PRACTICE

How good is your concentration? You can practise concentrating on court. Every time your mind wanders, tell yourself to think about hitting the ball. Focus on hitting the ball, getting ready for the next shot, and hitting the ball again. This is especially helpful during long groundstroke rallies.

Physical fitness

Tennis is a game of split-second reactions and quick sprints across the court. To play well, you need to be in good physical shape. As well as warming up before a match, it pays to keep fit, so you need to work out a training routine.

Diet for tennis

A healthy diet will give you the energy you need for tennis. The good news is that you can eat everything...in moderation, which does not mean having pizza or chips every day. Eat a good balance of carbohydrates (rice, pasta and bread), proteins (chicken and fish) and vitamins (fruit and veg). Stock up on carbohydrates before a match – they're your body's 'fuel'. But leave about two hours between eating and playing and drink plenty of fluids.

Warming down

After exercise, it's essential to warm down as this will stop your muscles aching the next day. Stretch your arms and legs and jog gently for 5 to 10 minutes.

The four Ss of fitness

The four Ss are the four areas of fitness which you need to work on to complement your technique. They are:

Speed – to reach the ball in time to play a good shot.
Suppleness – to bend, turn or jump to get into position.
Strength – to hit your shots with power.
Stamina – so you don't flake out halfway through a match!

Fit for tennis?

1 Speed

To test and improve your speed, try doing shuttle sprints across the width of the court. Place three balls on the singles sidelines, about a shoulder-width apart. Starting from the opposite sideline, sprint across court, pick up a ball, sprint back and put it down on the sideline.

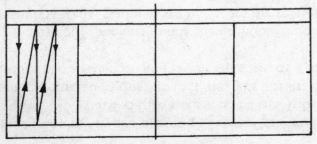

2 Suppleness

Stretching is a good way of improving suppleness. But make sure you warm up before you start. Hold each stretch for five seconds.

TRUNK ROTATION
Stand with your feet hip-width apart and your hands on your hips. Turn to your left, as far as possible and then turn to your right.

SIDE STRETCH
Stand with your feet hip-width apart, knees slightly bent. Raise one arm above your head and place the other hand on your hip. Bend to the side and hold. Straighten up, then repeat on the other side.

INNER THIGH

With your hands on your hips, bend one leg and stretch the other out behind you. Hold, then repeat with the other leg.

HAMSTRING STRETCH

Sit on the ground and stretch one leg out in front of you. Bend the other into your thigh, lean forward and try to touch your toes. Keep your back as straight as possible and repeat with the other leg.

THIGH STRETCH

Stand with your knees slightly bent. Hold your foot and pull it towards your bottom. Stretch out one arm, or lean against a wall for balance. Repeat with the other leg.

CALF STRETCH

Leaning against a wall, bend one knee and stretch your other leg out behind you, keeping the sole of your foot on the floor. Repeat with the other leg.

BACK STRETCH

Stand with your feet hip-width apart and your hands on your hips. Gently bend backwards as far as is comfortable.

3 Strength

These exercises will help build up your strength in your upper body, legs and stomach muscles. Do each one for 30 seconds, then rest. Gradually build up to longer.

PRESS-UPS

Lie face down with your hands beneath your shoulders. Using your arms, push your body up. Then lower your body almost to the ground, bending your elbows.

STANDING JUMPS

Stand with your feet slightly apart. Then jump up and forwards, bringing your knees up to your chest. Do this twice, rest and repeat.

SIT-UPS

Lie on your back, with your hand behind your head. Bend your knees, sit up and touch your knees with your elbows. Be careful not to wrench your neck forwards.

4 Stamina

Running and skipping are good ways of building up stamina. Start off by running for 5 minutes, walking for 5 minutes, running for 5 minutes and so on, for 30 minutes. Then build up to running for a longer period of time. Try doing 20 skips, then rest, do another 20 skips, and so on, up to 100 skips. You could also try swimming or cycling.

Tennis injuries

Injuries are the plague of a tennis player's life. To help you stay injury-free, warm up properly and don't overdo your training. One of the most common tennis injuries is called tennis elbow. This is when the muscles and tendons in your elbow become sore and inflamed. It can be caused by constantly mis-timing or mis-hitting your shots. As a general rule, if anything hurts, stop at once and allow plenty of time for injuries to heal.

Weight training

Top players build up and tone up their muscles by lifting weights in the gym, helping them to hit the ball harder and play more aggressively. Never try lifting weights yourself without professional instruction or guidance.

Taking things further

So if you dream of following in Tim Henman's footsteps and walking out to cheering crowds on Wimbledon Centre Court, how are you going to get there? There are various steps in getting to the top, but be warned, it can be a long and rocky road with no guarantees of making it. You'll need talent, determination and a large dose of luck. Still keen? Okay, let's see how to do it.

Starting off

A good place to start your tennis career is by playing in your school team. Get as much experience of match play as possible. You can also join a tennis club – contact your national tennis association for details of your local club. Once there, sign up for any group coaching sessions on offer.

Finding a coach

The next stage is to find a coach for one-to-one coaching. Ask at your local club – they may have their own tennis professional, or contact your national association for a list of registered coaches. It's essential to find a coach you get on with. He or she should be tough but encouraging and be able to make practising fun. Book one lesson to start with to see how you get on.

Going to tournaments

When you're ready, your coach will advise you about entering tournaments, which may be held locally or nationally. If you join your national association's ranking scheme, you'll be given a 'rating' or score based on your level of play. This allows you to enter 'ratings tournaments' where you'll be drawn against players of a similar rating, at least in the first stages of play. As your results improve, so will your rating.

Professional tennis

If everything goes according to plan, you may want to become a professional player, right up there with the Rafters and Kournikovas. After all, this could be your big chance to earn pots of cash and be treated like a film star. But competition is tough at the top and very few players make it. Those who do, join the professional tour.

Going on tour

The men's tour is called the ATP (Association of Tennis Professionals) Tour and the women's tour is called the WTA (Women's Tennis Association) Tour. Each consists of the top tournaments around the world. Players earn points for all matches won and the further they progress and the higher the prize money, the more points they win. It is possible to earn bonus points for beating higher-ranked players and these points are fed into a computer to work out the player's world ranking.

Seeding

In most tournaments, the top players are 'seeded' or ranked according to how well they have been playing. Seedings are usually based on the players' computer rankings. Seeding is a way of making sure that the best players meet in the later stages of the tournament.

Books and magazines

There are lots of books around with tips on techniques and playing matches. Here are some suggestions to start with:

The Handbook of Tennis
Paul Douglas
Pelham Books
Takes you step-by-step through each shot with tips on improving your strokes, practice drills and singles and doubles tactics.

Top Coach Tennis
Mark Cox and Charles Applewhaite
Macdonald Queen Anne Press
Written by one of Britain's most successful players and one of Britain's top coaches, this book is packed with information.

The Junior Tennis Handbook
Skip Singleton
Shoe Tree Press
A complete guide for junior players by a leading American coach. Clearly and simply written.

Tennis for Dummies
Patrick McEnroe
IDG Books
A fun guide to the game by John's less well-known brother.

Magazines

Search your newsagent's shelves for tennis magazines – there are plenty around. Look for names like *Tennis Week* and *Tennis World*.

To subscribe to *Ace*, the official monthly magazine of the British LTA, telephone 0171 381 7037 or write to:

Ace
9-11 North End Road
London W14 8ST

Useful addresses

For helpful advice, try contacting the following organisations:

The Lawn Tennis Association (LTA)
The Queen's Club
West Kensington
London W14 9EG
Tel: 0171 381 7000

International Tennis Federation
Bank Lane
Roehampton
London SW15 5XZ
Tel: 0181 878 6464

National Wheelchair Tennis Association
65 Overlea Drive
Hawarden
Clywd CH5 3HS
Tel: 01244 533111

Tennis Australia
Private Bag 6060
Richmond South
Victoria 3121
Australia

Fédération Française de Tennis
Stade Roland Garros
2 Avenue Gordon Bennett
75016 Paris
France

United States Tennis Association (USTA)
70 West Red Oak Lane
White Plains
New York NY 10604
USA

Fan Clubs

Write off for newsletters, posters and signed photos of your favourite stars!

Topspin (The Official Tim Henman Fan Club)
PO Box 2448
Reading, Berks RG4 6YE

G-Force (The Official Greg Rusedski Fan Club)
PO Box 16856
London SE21 8WP

Baseline (Andre Agassi)
227 Henley Road
Caversham
Reading, Berks RG4 6LJ

PR Unlimited (The Official Pat Rafter Fan Club)
181 Citadel Road
The Hoe
Plymouth, Devon PL1 2HU

Going to the net

Talking of nets... There are lots of tennis websites on the Internet, packed with fascinating facts about the men's and women's tours, when and where the top tournaments are played and, most importantly, how to get tickets. Here are a few to check out:

http://www.wimbledon.org
Packed with information about the Wimbledon Championships in London, with results as they happen and advice on how to get tickets.

http://www.ausopen.org
All about the Australian Open in Melbourne, including how to apply for tickets.

http://www.frenchopen.org
A brilliant site full of information about the French Open in Paris, including lots about the history of the tournament.

http://www.usopen.org
Experience the unique atmosphere of the US Open in New York from the comfort of your own home!

http://www.lta.org
The official website of the Lawn Tennis Association of Britain.

http://www.usta.org
The official website of the United States Tennis Association. A good place to go to look up the rules.

http://www.aptour.com
http://www.corelwtatour.com
The latest news from the men's (ATP) and women's (WTA) professional tours.

http://itftennis.com
The official website of the International Tennis Federation, the world governing body of tennis.

The Rules of Tennis

This is a summary of the main rules of tennis. For the full rules, look up the United States Tennis Association website (http://usta.org). Many rules have already been explained in this book. The relevant page numbers are given in brackets.

Rules 1 & 2: The court and net (pages 16–18)

Rule 3: The ball
- Balls must be yellow or white, between 6.35-6.67 cm in diameter and 56.7-58.5 g in weight.

Rule 4: The racket
- The frame must not be more than 81.28 cm long, including the handle, and 31.75 cm wide. The stringed area must not be more than 39.37 cm long and 29.21 cm wide.

Rule 5: The server and receiver
- The players stand on either side of the net. The one who first plays the ball is the server; the other is the receiver.

Rule 6: Choice of ends (page 20)

Rule 7: The service (pages 38–45)

Rule 8: Foot faults (page 41)

Rule 9: Delivery of service
- The server serves first from the right court, then alternately from the right and left courts. If he serves from the wrong side by mistake, the point stands but the next ball must be served from the correct side.

Rule 10: Service fault
The service is a fault if:
- the server misses the ball as he tries to hit it
- the ball touches a permanent fixture (apart from the net, strap or band) before it hits the ground.

Rule 11: Second serve (page 43)

Rule 12: When to serve
- The server should not serve until the receiver is ready.

Rules 13 & 14: The let (page 41)

Rule 15: Order of service
- At the end of the first game, the receiver becomes the server and the server the receiver.

Rule 16: Changing ends (page 44)

Rule 17: The ball in play
- The ball is in play from the service until the point is decided.

Rule 18: Server wins point
- If the ball touches the receiver or his clothing before it hits the ground.
- If the receiver loses the point as in Rule 20.

Rule 19: Receiver wins point
- If the server serves a double fault (page 41).

Taking things further

- If the server loses the point as in Rule 20.

Rule 20: Players lose points

- If the ball bounces twice before they hit it.
- If the ball lands out of court (page 18).
- If they catch or carry the ball on their racket or hit it twice.
- If their racket or clothing touches the net or ground in their opponent's court while the ball is in play.
- If they volley the ball before it crosses the net.
- If the ball touches them or their clothing.
- If they throw their racket at the ball.

Rule 21: Players hinder opponents

- If players deliberately prevent opponents playing a stroke, they lose the point. If it is an accident, the point is replayed.

Rule 22: Ball falls on line

- If the ball hits the line, it is in (page 18).

Rule 23: Ball touches a fixture

- If the ball hits a fixture such as the umpire's chair before it bounces, the opponent then wins the point.

Rule 24: A good return

It is a good return if:
- The ball touches the net, goes over and lands in court.
- The ball goes over the net, then rebounds or is blown back over and the player whose turn it is to play reaches over and hits the ball (provided that his body or clothes do not touch the net).
- The ball is returned outside the posts or singles sticks and still lands in.
- A player's racket goes over the net after he hits the ball, provided that he hit the ball on his own side of the net.

Rule 25: Hindrance of a player

- If a player is stopped from playing by something outside his control such as a ball rolling on court, a 'let' is called. If the server has already served on fault, he takes two serves (the whole point is replayed, not just the stroke).

Rules 26-28: Scoring (page 20)

Rule 29: Role of court officials (page 19)

Rule 30: Continuous play

Play must be continuous from the first serve until the end of the match, according to the following rules:
- If the first serve is a fault, then the server must immediately serve again.
- When changing ends, a maximum of 90 seconds rest is allowed.
- If a player is injured accidentally, the umpire may allow one three-minute break for treatment.
- The umpire can penalise a player for deliberately holding up play.

Rule 31: Coaching
- In some team competitions, players may receive coaching from the team captain when changing ends.
- In any other match, coaching is not allowed.

Rule 32: Changing balls
(page 13)

Rule 33: Rules for doubles
- The same rules apply for singles and doubles, except for those listed below.

Rule 34: The court (pages 16–17)

Rule 35: Order of service
- The order of serving can be decided at the start of each set.
- The serving pair decide who will serve first. The other player serves in the third game.

Rule 36: Order of receiving
- The order of receiving can be decided at the start of each set.
- The receivers decide who will receive first, and alternate throughout each game.

Rule 37: Service out of turn
- If a player serves out of turn, the correct player serves as soon as the mistake is discovered. Any points already scored stand. If a whole game is completed, the order of service stays as altered.

Rule 38: Receiving out of turn
- If the wrong person receives, the order stays altered until the end of game but goes back to normal for the next game.

Rule 39: Service faults
- The serve is a fault if it breaks Rule 10 or if the ball touches the server's partner or his clothing.
- If the ball touches the receiver's partner before it hits the ground, the server wins the point.

Rule 40: Playing the ball
- The ball must be hit by each team in turn.

Glossary

Approach shot A shot used to put your opponent on the defensive so that you can go to the net to volley.

Australian formation A tactical doubles formation. Both the server and server's partner stand on the same side of the court.

Backhand A shot played to the left of the body by right-handed players, and to the right of the body by left-handers.

Backspin Another word for slice. You hit down and under the ball to make it spin backwards and keep low after bouncing.

Baseliner A player with strong groundstrokes who likes to play from the back of the court.

Chip and charge A tactic which uses a sliced ('chipped') shot to allow you to charge into the net.

Chopper grip The grip you use for serves, volleys and smashes. You hold the racket as you would an axe or 'chopper'.

Closed face When the face of the racket is angled so that it faces down towards the court.

Cross-court shot A shot which is played diagonally across the court.

Double-handed backhand A backhand shot played with both hands on the racket for extra power and control.

Drive A groundstroke played on either the backhand or forehand side, deep into your opponent's court.

Drive volley A volley played like a drive, but before the ball has bounced.

Drop shot A shot played lightly with slice so that it just drops over the net and stays low as it bounces.

Drop volley A volley played like a drop shot but before the ball has bounced. It lands close to the net and bounces low.

Eastern grip The grip you use to play a forehand, holding the racket as if you are shaking hands. The 'V' between your thumb and index finger is slightly to the right, or east, on the racket handle.

Foot fault If your foot touches the baseline or the inside of the court before you hit the serve.

Forehand A shot played to the right of the body by right-handed players, and to the left of the body by left-handers.

Groundstroke A shot played after the ball has bounced with a long, swinging action, for example a forehand or backhand drive.

Half-volley A shot where you hit the ball just after it bounces.

Knock-up The few minutes before a match when you practise your shots on court with your opponent.

Let When a point is replayed, for example if there is interference during a rally (such as a ball rolling across court) or if a serve hits the net cord but lands in.

No-man's land The zone of the court between the service line and the baseline. If you get stranded in no-man's land it can be difficult to hit good shots during a rally.

Open face When the face of the racket is angled so that it is turned up and away from the court.

Overhead A shot played over your head, for example, a serve or a smash.

Passing shot A shot used to go past your opponent when he or she is at the net.

Percentage tennis Shots which have the highest percentage, that is, are most likely to land safely in court to cut down on unnecessary errors.

Poaching A doubles tactic in which the net player moves across the net to his partner's side to play a volley.

Rally An exchange of shots between the players.

Semi-western grip The grip you use to play a topspin forehand. You hold the racket to the left, or west, on the handle. For a full western grip, you hold the racket further round to the left.

Serve, service The shot used to put the ball in play at the beginning of a point. You have two attempts to get the serve into court.

Serve-and-volleyer A player who likes to run in after his or her serve and volley at the net.

Slice Another word for backspin. You hit down and under the ball to make it spin backwards and keep low after bouncing.

Smash A shot played over your head, hitting the ball down hard.

Stop volley A volley played so that you take the pace (speed) off the ball and drop it just over the net.

Sweet spot The spot near the centre of the racket face which gives your shots maximum power and accuracy.

Tennis elbow A common injury caused by mis-hitting or mis-timing the ball. Your elbow becomes sore and inflamed.

Titanium A strong, light metal used to make some rackets.

Topspin When you hit up and over the ball to give it extra speed and control and make it kick forward after bouncing.

Touch shot A delicate shot played with great control rather than power.

Volley A short, sharp shot played before the ball bounces with a punching action.

Wrong-footing Playing the ball back to a spot on the court from which your opponent has just moved.

Index

All you need to know

0 340 773294	Acting	£3.99	☐
0 340 764686	Athletics	£3.99	☐
0 340 736305	Basketball	£3.99	☐
0 340 715189	Cartooning	£3.99	☐
0 340 736496	Chess	£3.99	☐
0 340 715200	Computers Unlimited	£3.99	☐
0 340 736275	Cricket	£3.99	☐
0 340 715219	Drawing	£3.99	☐
0 340 736313	Film-making	£3.99	☐
0 340 736291	Fishing	£3.99	☐
0 340 715138	Football	£3.99	☐
0 340 76466X	Golf	£3.99	☐
0 340 778970	Gymnastics	£3.99	☐
0 340 736321	In-line Skating	£3.99	☐
0 340 749504	Karate	£3.99	☐
0 340 715146	The Internet	£3.99	☐
0 340 736267	Memory Workout	£3.99	☐
0 340 736283	Pop Music	£3.99	☐
0 340 715170	Riding	£3.99	☐
0 340 736518	Rugby	£3.99	☐
0 340 715235	Skateboarding	£3.99	☐
0 340 736526	Snowboarding	£3.99	☐
0 340 71512X	Swimming	£3.99	☐
0 340 764465	Tennis	£3.99	☐
0 340 773332	Writing	£3.99	☐
0 340 73650X	Your Own Website	£3.99	☐

Turn the page to find out how to order these books.

ORDER FORM

Books in the **super.activ** series are available at your local bookshop, or can be ordered direct from the publisher. A complete list of titles is given on the previous page. Just tick the titles you would like and complete the details below. Prices and availability are subject to change without prior notice.

Please enclose a cheque or postal order made payable to Bookpoint Ltd, and send to: Hodder Children's Books, Cash Sales Dept, Bookpoint, 39 Milton Park, Abingdon, Oxon OX14 4TD. Email address: orders@bookpoint.co.uk.

If you would prefer to pay by credit card, our call centre team would be delighted to take your order by telephone. Our direct line is 01235 400414 (lines open 9.00 am – 6.00 pm, Monday to Saturday; 24-hour message answering service). Alternatively you can send a fax on 01235 400454.

Title .... First name .... Surname ....

Address ....

....

....

Daytime tel .... Postcode....................................

If you would prefer to post a credit card order, please complete the following.

Please debit my Visa/Access/Diner's Card/American Express (delete as applicable) card number:

Signature ....Expiry Date ....

If you would NOT like to receive further information on our products, please tick ☐ .